KABBALAH ON THE Sabbath

© 2008 Kabbalah Centre International, Inc.

Kabbalah Publishing is a registered DBA of
Kabbalah Centre International, Inc.

For further information:

The Kabbalah Centre
155 E. 48th St., New York, NY 10017
1062 S. Robertson Blvd., Los Angeles, CA 90035

1.800.Kabbalah www.kabbalah.com

First Edition
September 2008
Printed in Canada
ISBN10: 1-57189-602-3
ISBN13: 978-1-57189-602-5

Design: HL Design (Hyun Min Lee) www.hldesignco.com

KABBALAH ON THE
Sabbath

YEHUDA BERG

TABLE OF CONTENTS

ACKNOWLEDGMENTS

To the people who make my life better each and every day: my parents, the Rav and Karen; my brother Michael; my wife Michal and our children.

Chapter One

More Than Just a Day of Rest

The Bible tells us God required six days to create the universe, and then one day to rest from that labor. This day is known as the Sabbath, or *Shabbat* in Hebrew. Israelites believe this day of rest is on Saturday. Christians observe it on Sunday. Muslims designate the Sabbath on Friday.

So why do we think God couldn't whip up a universe instantly? Or that God needs to rest? And if God created the entire universe, including the seven days of the week, why is only one day holy? If God created them, shouldn't every day be holy? Are we to conclude that God sometimes holds back when creating something? If so, why? If I were building a home for my family, and had unlimited resources, I can't imagine building the seventh room using only the finest workmanship and premium materials, and then scrimping on the other six. What would be the point?

The Day of Rest

And if the Sabbath is the day of rest, why does no one seem to be resting? During the Sabbath, the secular world is out at the mall shopping, or in the park attending the children's soccer games. For some, those who do observe the Sabbath, it sometimes seems more about socializing than about rejuvenation. In Kabbalah Centres around the world, the Sabbath is the longest day of the week we "work" from sundown Friday night to sundown Saturday evening. So why does the Sabbath still have this reputation of being a *day of rest*? For most of us, every day is an uphill struggle in our never-ending quest to find some happiness; which leads to a question: why didn't God just create paradise to begin with? Why create a being called Adam who sins and falls into a dark, dangerous world where lasting happiness and enduring fulfillment are as rare as unicorns? Why create a world where sin is even an option, much less a constant temptation?

What's the Point of it All?

The Sabbath, according to Kabbalah, serves a specific purpose that has nothing to do with religion, tradition, worship, rest, or conventional prayer. What is it? For now, let me give you the condensed version. Later, we'll explore the technology of the Sabbath in much greater detail (and reveal some compelling kabbalistic secrets that have been hidden for centuries).

The ancient kabbalists tell us that during the so-called Six Days of Creation, God created the Earth, animals, mountains, trees, and humankind. However, all this creative output existed only in a state of potential. In fact, say the kabbalists, during this six-day period the world was not yet alive. It was only on the seventh day that an infusion of energy, or Light, surged through God's Creation, bringing it out of its state of suspended animation and into existence. This insight begins to open us to the meaning of the Sabbath, and to the Light it can bring into our lives.

Let's look at it another way. If you've studied in a Kabbalah Centre or read any of our books you know the ancient Kabbalists tell us that all life, including all physical matter, is based on three fundamental forces of energy a positive force (+), a negative force (-), and a neutral mediating force. This *Three Column System* is the foundation of both the spiritual system and the physical universe. As you might imagine, two thousand years ago this was a very strange-sounding description of the basic structure of reality. Today, thanks to the wonders of modern science, we can recognize these three forces as the proton, electron, and neutron. These are the subatomic particles that join together to create the atom, the building block of the world as we know it. Increasingly, we're finding that such discoveries of modern science support ideas that kabbalists were enunciating several thousand years earlier.

Kabbalists tell us that these three forces took their final form on the seventh day of Creation, prior to which they existed only in a state of potential. On the seventh day, some atoms joined together to build mountains, lakes and forests. Others produced the vegetable and animal kingdoms. And still other atoms combined to create humankind.

Of course, this did not happen in a day. According to the kabbalists, *day* is a code word, as are many other words in the Torah, or Old Testament. The point I wish to make is this: Every Sabbath contains the original energy of the seventh day of Creation. And this means that on every Sabbath we have the ability to transform our reality, to change everything *at the atomic level.* Every week, on this one day, we can alter our physical environment personally and globally using the power of Sabbath energy.

When we truly understand this technology the Sabbath will become not part of a religious tradition followed in order to receive the Creator's blessings, but the ultimate tool for transforming our world. This traditional approach has failed us for millennia: our chaotic world certainly does not look or feel blessed. The simple reason for this chaos is that, over time, we have reduced a powerful technology to the status of mere religion. The intent of this book is to replace dogmatic or habitual behavior with genuine understanding, and a deep appreciation for the power of the Sabbath as a gift to *all* humankind.

From Slave to King

The great Kabbalist Rav Nachman of Breslav describes the Sabbath by using the analogy of a king and a slave. He says that as humans our typical state of consciousness is all about taking receiving. It's about getting as much as we can in order to satisfy our endless stream of desires. We are in this incessant *taking mode*, kabbalists explain, because we are always in a state of lack. Like a slave with limited ability to fill his or her own desires, we see ourselves as dependent on the good will of others, begging to be given what we want out of life.

A king, however, already has everything he could possibly want. And on the Sabbath, says Rav Nachman, we are like the king. The Creator gives us everything. The vaults are open to all the treasures in the universe that are stored in the Upper Worlds (the 99 Percent Reality from which this world derived), and we are all invited to help ourselves to these infinite riches.

The *Zohar*, the sacred text of Kabbalah, says that during the Sabbath everyone is filled with Light that replaces one's sorrows and despair. In both the Upper and Lower Worlds, the 1 Percent and 99 Percent, there is only happiness. On the Sabbath, the Creator actually goes into the *Garden of Eden*, where all the souls and all the angels in the Upper Worlds spend the Sabbath joyfully together. Everyone receives this gift during the Sabbath, even if unaware of it, and once we do become aware of this technology we can learn how to benefit from its inconceivable power.

The great 18th century Kabbalist Rav Israel Ben Eliezer, known as the Baal Shem Tov (*Master of the Good Name*) tells us that a man who has limped since childhood might, while still relatively young, have hope that one day he'll overcome his affliction. But if he is still limping when he's an old man, he knows he will limp for the remainder of his days. He no longer carries the hope that things can change.

But what if once a week he lost his limp? Suddenly he would have good reason to continue to believe that one day his limp could be overcome for good. The Baal Shem Tov tells us that once a week, on the Sabbath, every man, woman and child on Earth no longer limps. On the Sabbath, we return to our fully perfected selves, to the union of all our souls that existed before the creation of chaos, darkness, and death. My father, Kabbalist Rav Berg (whom we call *the Rav*, which means *the Teacher*) always says that the Sabbath is not *holy* but "*wholly*," because it connects us to the whole— the perfect reality and blissful world that lies beyond our five senses. The biblical sages of history have often said that the Sabbath is a taste of the *World to Come*.

Rav Ashlag, the greatest Kabbalist of the 20th century and the founder of The Kabbalah Centre, explains that the so-called *World to Come* does not refer to some heavenly place that we will discover or experience after death, or at the End of Days, as is often assumed. Rather, it refers to the spiritual dimensions from which the Light and Energy of the Creator springs eternally. The Sabbath is our point of entry into those hidden dimensions. More than that, the Sabbath allows us to bring those hidden dimensions into our personal lives any time we choose. The ideal is to bring the *World to Come* into the here and now, and the Sabbath provides us a way to do just that.

According to the kabbalists, every action we take is like a seed. If we plant negative seeds, intentionally or not, the fruits that materialize in our lives are negative. This is why chaos strikes. On the other hand, positive actions plant seeds of a wholly different kind. Their fruit brings us our moments of happiness and good fortune. When everything goes right in life, it is a direct result of our positive actions in the past.

The Sabbath supplies Light and Energy for the seeds we plant, to ensure they are strong, healthy, and positive. This Light also nourishes the fruits that appear as a result of those seeds. How does the Sabbath accomplish all this? To answer this question, I need to give you a brief introduction to what Kabbalah tells us about the creation of the world and the purpose of life.

Chapter Two

With Questions Come Answers

THE POINT OF CREATION

In the very beginning, God created perfection, a reality of endless happiness. You and I were part of that perfect state, but still something deep within us made us feel less than fully complete. Because we were made of the same Light as God, we shared God's desire to give; what we wanted was the ability to create this perfection ourselves. So we asked God for the opportunity to do so. In response, God then took this perfect realm of pure Light, infinite wisdom, and incalculable happiness, and made it *imperfect*.

How? By dividing it up and hiding the Light, wisdom, and happiness behind a curtain. The curtain is the reason we find ourselves today in a dark and dangerous universe. It is the reason we are no longer continuously embraced by the infinite Light. In fact, we don't even remember that it exists. According to Kabbalah, we now have an opportunity to create perfection in our lives and in the world by pulling back the curtain.

To recap: Once upon a time there was utter perfection. This perfection was dismantled, creating imperfection. Human beings were given the opportunity to put the Original Realm back together again so that they could embody the joy of creating perfection. Just like God.

CREATING IMPERFECTION

According to Kabbalah, as you can see, God created imperfection because you and I asked for it. We don't remember this because forgetting all about our origins is part of the imperfection in which we now live. Rediscovering where we originally came from (as you are doing this very moment) is part of what recreating perfection is all about.

So why can't you perceive the transformation from imperfection to perfection taking place within you right now as you absorb these words? Your five senses are imperfect, that's why. They deceive you. They don't show you the whole picture. Nonetheless, you *are* bringing yourself and this world closer to perfection as you read these words and grasp the wisdom they convey. Coming to understand and appreciate this wisdom is the beauty and power of learning Kabbalah. Let me explain.

The Power of Learning Kabbalah

When you study history, you become smarter, intellectually speaking. It's the same with geography, science, and math. A person becomes more knowledgeable as he or she reads into a particular subject. But that person's state of consciousness remains the same. The individual has acquired additional information, but has not increased his or her level of spiritual and physical awareness. From that perspective, nothing has changed. When you study Kabbalah (and learn the secrets of the universe), you become not just wiser but purer; you move your body, your soul, and all of humankind closer to perfection.

You don't have to take my word for it. And according to Kabbalah, you shouldn't. Kabbalah encourages us to question authority. The Rav always likes to say that he is from Missouri, also known as "The Show Me State." You could say that all kabbalists, dating back four thousand years to Abraham himself, were from Missouri, in a sense: all of them tell us not to accept even a single word of Kabbalah instruction or a single principle on faith alone. On the contrary, we should always test ideas to see if they work for us.

The Power of Perfection

You might be wondering what the *perfection* Kabbalah describes as its goal means on a practical level. It means this: The absolute end of all chaos, pain, darkness—and even of death itself. The only reason we find it so difficult to believe in the possibility of a world without death is because we are still imperfect. It's a Catch 22, and the only way out is to learn—and live— the wisdom of Kabbalah. The results speak for themselves. You don't have to take anyone's word for it. When you apply the technology of Kabbalah, you *experience* the increase in perfection in your own personal life.

The End of Concealment

By unraveling the mysteries of the Sabbath—the reason for its existence, its function, its purpose—you and the world will take a quantum leap toward ultimate perfection. Paradoxically, perhaps, learning all about how God created our state of *imperfection* actually helps us move toward perfection itself. So every time you learn another concept, dropping into place another piece of the spiritual puzzle, you pull yourself another step out of darkness.

So let's get to it. Let's start acquiring knowledge and mastering some illuminating concepts about life, the human soul, spirituality, and the Sabbath. Perfection has been waiting a long time to return to our lives, so let's not postpone it any longer.

FROM PERFECT TO IMPERFECT

Before there were *days*, before there were *weeks*, *months*, or *years*, even before the sun and Earth gave rise to years, months, weeks and days, there, physically speaking, was nothing at all. The only thing that existed was a single Thought, which we will call *consciousness*. Consciousness is a vastly misunderstood word. According to Kabbalah, consciousness is a force of energy pregnant with intelligence. The Rav often refers to it as *Energy-Intelligence*.

Kabbalistic cosmology tells us that this Force of Consciousness is infinite. Endless. The ancient kabbalists called it *Light*. Why Light? Because the phenomenon on Earth that behaves most like this original Force of Consciousness is the light of the sun. Merely by its presence, sunlight instantly banishes darkness from a room. Darkness cannot coexist with sunlight. Sunlight also expands instantly, filling every inch of space. It gives us life. It sustains our entire planet. Without the light of the sun there is no photosynthesis. No life. And sunlight contains all the colors of the rainbow, plus the millions of different colors that these seven colors are able to generate when they combine together in different ways.

Before the beginning, the Infinite Force, which we call Light, filled eternity. There was no darkness anywhere to be found. Every conceivable form of happiness was like a color of the rainbow within this unending expanse of blazing Light. Unlike sunlight, the Light contained an incalculable amount of knowledge and wisdom. What I'm describing are not primary or secondary features of the Light: the measureless wisdom, the unlimited pleasure, the infinite happiness, and the eternal life-giving power were all one single Force.

The Ultimate Source

If you look around today you'll see examples of the Light everywhere: music, theater, books, stories, films, architectural achievements, scientific discoveries, life-changing technologies, transportation—the list goes on and on. Everything we see in this world that is positive, productive, and fulfilling was contained in this original Light. Human beings merely give expression to these wonders, acting as channels to reveal this Light in our physical reality. Even these words I've written are part of the Light, as is your ability to read and understand them.

Infinite Stillness

Another remarkable feature of this Realm of Consciousness was that it contained no space. The Light filled everything. Nor was there movement of any kind. Why? When Light fills everything, there is no place for anything to go anywhere; everything is everywhere at once. I know, this isn't easy to imagine. But if you lived in such a world, every kind of happiness, pleasure, knowledge and joy would be at your disposal instantly. Effortlessly. Infinitely. As noted, but worth repeating, the reason we find ourselves in this world instead, Kabbalah explains, is because it is God's response to our desire to experience the joy of creating perfection ourselves.

Chapter Three

Creating the Illusion of Imperfection

FROM FLAWLESSNESS TO DEFICIENCY

To satisfy our desire to become like God, the Creator had to figure out a way to create imperfection out of the luminous perfection that permeated all reality. In truth, this was an impossible task—even for God. Why? Simple logic tells us that if perfection is truly perfect, then it is not subject to being undone. So God had to figure out a way to create the *illusion* of imperfection. That's what all the chaos of our current daily lives really is—an illusion.

Consider the light of the sun. Darkness has no place in sunlight; thus sunlight can never produce it. However, we can create the illusion of darkness by giving rise to a space where sunlight cannot enter. This is sort of what God did. By hanging up curtains to dim the effect of the Light, God created the illusion of imperfection in the small, dark, temporary space that would become our universe.

THE *OPPOSITE* ILLUSION

There are a number of significant implications—beyond just creating darkness—that arise when one blocks out both sunlight and God's Light. By hanging up a curtain to prevent sunlight from entering into a room, you literally create a state of existence that seems to be the opposite of the reality outside the room. This is the principle at work in our universe. The divine blackout curtains that God set up created a reality that appears to be the opposite of the infinite Realm of Consciousness and Light—in every conceivable way. Let's examine the original Realm of Light in order to understand what its opposite would look like in our world.

THE REALM OF LIGHT	CURTAIN	OPPOSITE WORLD
Light		Darkness
Energy		Matter
Motionless		Motion
Timelessness		Time
No Space		Space
Happy		Sad
Immortality		Death
Truth		Lies
Wisdom		Ignorance
Divinity		Godlessness
Good		Evil
Oneness		Diversity
Consciousness being the root of all reality		Physical matter and laws devoid of Consciousness and purpose

Alice in Wonderland

When we take a moment to examine the list above we see that it contains some profound ideas. According to Kabbalah, we are like Alice who fell into the looking glass in Lewis Carroll's *Alice in Wonderland*. We see and experience the opposite of what is actually there. Unfortunately, this makes life quite a daunting proposition, because even *truth* is temporarily missing from this world. Instead of reality we are immersed in speculation, superstitions, myths, legends, falsehoods, and delusions about the meaning (or meaninglessness) of life itself.

Let's explore a few.

Immortality

Consider the idea of eternal existence. As we've seen, *immortality* is part of the true reality from which everything originated. Yet all we see in our world are graveyards, funerals, murder, disease, and sickness. We're weighed down by evidence that death is the one thing we can count on in this life, when in fact, according to Kabbalah, death is a fleeting phenomenon; it only looks permanent because our brains have been wired to accept the illusion in which we live.

If we limit ourselves to what we can confirm from our own experience, we have to admit that we have no idea what's really happening on the other side of the curtain when someone leaves this physical reality. From the perspective of the deceased, it is we who've disappeared from their view, so perhaps they are alive and it is we who are dead. Ideas such as these are difficult to even consider because of the curtain, which keeps us in ignorance.

A Realm Without Time

Consider the concept of time. Since most physicists are not kabbalists, they are dumbfounded by the discovery that on a subatomic level of existence, time moves *both* ways. That's right, scientists have established that time is reversible in the microscopic world of molecules and subatomic particles; it moves forward and backwards.

But in the world we perceive with our five senses, time only moves one way—*forward!*

That's a problem for us. Why? Because a glass shatters but does not repair itself. Our hot morning coffee cools down by itself, but it will never heat itself up. This one-way flow of time causes entropy—the tendency of systems to lose energy, or deteriorate over time. In our world things wear out and never repair themselves. Everything around us is in constant decay, including our bodies. We grow old and sometimes sick, and then we die.

Today's physicists are still scratching their collective heads in bewilderment, wondering how a microscopic reality in which time flows both ways could also provide the building blocks for our world—a dimension where time only flows one way. This conundrum is called the *time reversibility paradox*. In other words, if molecules can go forward and backwards in time, and you and I are made up of molecules, why can't we do the same thing? Questions like this led Albert Einstein to declare, "Reality is an illusion, albeit a persistent one."

Kabbalah tells us that Einstein was right. What we consider reality *is* an illusion, including time. It's the opposite of *no time* because we're inside the mirror, in a world that projects the reverse of true reality. Like darkness, it is the curtain that creates the illusion of time moving only one way. We can reverse death and the arrow of time simply by connecting ourselves to the true reality. And the Sabbath provides us with that connection.

When scientists explore the subatomic world, they are getting closer to true reality. They are approaching the mirror and looking through it, just a little bit. This is why the quantum subatomic world of protons, electrons, and neutrons appears to behave so strangely. If physicists probe a little deeper (to the other side of the curtain, or mirror) they will realize there is no such thing as time at all.

As we move away from the subatomic realm, the layers of curtain naturally increase and the illusion of time becomes more and more tangible. By the time you reach the world as we perceive it with our five senses, the state of zero time has been left behind completely. This also works in reverse. If enough curtains could be removed, time—and with it, aging—could be slowed down. If even more curtains were taken down, aging could come to a halt; time would disappear. How's that for an ambitious agenda?

As we will soon discover in greater detail, the ego is the primary curtain that separates us from the Light. The bigger the ego, the greater the curtain—and the greater the distance we find ourselves from true reality.

Physical Matter

Matter, according to Kabbalah, is also an illusion perpetuated by the curtain. On one side of the curtain there is spiritual energy or Light. On the other side we find what appears to be its opposite—*physical matter.* The energy on one side of the curtain, as we have discussed, is actually made up of consciousness. So if physical matter is the opposite of true reality it must be devoid of consciousness—or seem to be. In truth, matter is merely consciousness in a *frozen state*. This being the case, kabbalists tell us our thoughts are much closer to true reality than our physical bodies.

Once we tap into this deep understanding, we begin to see how consciousness can control physical matter. Mind over matter is true reality because mind *is* matter. Consciousness creates the mind and consciousness creates matter. Now we can see clearly that all illnesses, for instance, are a direct result of our state of consciousness.

CAUSE AND EFFECT

Our entire world operates according to the law of *Cause and Effect*. When you plant a seed, the seed represents the Cause; when a tree or fruit appears, that is the Effect. Kabbalah says there are no random occurrences in life. Everything that happens has a seed, or Cause. Even though it is hidden from view, the true reality—the Realm of Light—on the other side of the curtain is the ultimate Cause, and our physical world is the Effect. On this side of the curtain we never actually perceive the Original Cause; it remains hidden to us, but it is still there. This is important to understand.

Suppose you plant an apple seed in the ground, and over time it grows into a tree. Can you still see the original seed? No. Of course not. Once the Effect (the tree) appears, the Original Cause is no longer visible. This is why it is so hard for us to see our own true origins. The seed, or Cause, that gave birth to our physical world (the Effect) is hidden. It vanished, just as an apple seed does once the root, trunk and branches of the sapling begin to appear.

How, then, are we to discover the absolute Cause of all Causes?

Finding the Cause

We have, in our possession, a powerful kabbalistic method for discovering the true cause of everything. The great kabbalists of antiquity revealed this technique by way of a simple but profound kabbalistic insight.

- *The Cause Always Contains the Effect, and the Effect Always Contains the Cause*

Once again, consider our apple tree. An apple seed is the Cause, and the apple tree is the Effect. Why doesn't a pear tree spring from an apple seed? Because the Cause—the apple seed—*also* contains the Effect—*the full-blown apple tree!* This explains the first half of the above insight—*The Cause Always Contains the Effect.*

Now let's examine the second half: *the Effect Always Contains the Cause.* The final Effect of an apple seed is the fruit (a juicy apple) dangling at the tip of the branch on the apple tree. Kabbalah says *the Effect contains the Cause.* As we've discussed, once an apple tree begins to grow, the Original Cause—the Seed—virtually disappears. However, if you peek inside the apple fruit (the ultimate Effect) you will find the Original Cause—*another apple seed.* This leads us to a very important conclusion: by examining the final Effect, one can extrapolate the Cause of anything, even though the original Cause itself is no longer visible.

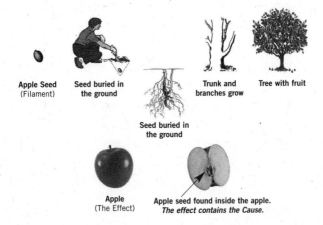

Apple Seed
(Filament)

Seed buried in the ground

Seed buried in the ground

Trunk and branches grow

Tree with fruit

Apple
(The Effect)

Apple seed found inside the apple.
The effect contains the Cause.

The Seed Contains the Purpose/Consciousness

There's one more thing we need to know. The consciousness or intelligence in an apple seed has a specific intention—to create an apple tree. Thus, when we find the Effect, we also find its *purpose*, which is to create that *final Effect*. Staying with the apple tree example, we have just discovered that delving into the final Effect reveals both the hidden Cause and the purpose behind the manifestation of the actual Effect.

If we take this principle and apply it to our own circumstances, we should be able to discover the meaning of life, the Cause of our existence, and our purpose.

Finding the Hidden Cause of all Causes

Since we live in the imperfect world on this side of the curtain, the original Cause and Purpose of Creation is invisible to us—just like the apple seed that has vanished by the time the tree emerges. We cannot see it or sense it with our imperfect brain and five senses. However, if we employ the kabbalistic science of Cause and Effect we can discover the Cause–and purpose—of existence: all we need do is look at the Effect of existence and peek inside to see what it contains.

The Ultimate Effect

If a fruit is the Effect of a seed in the vegetable kingdom, it is humankind—specifically a man and a woman—that represents the final Effect in the human kingdom. Just as an apple contains a seed (the Cause), humankind also contains a seed inside our human reproductive organs, which itself contains the Cause of our existence. In a man it is the sperm, and in a woman it is the egg. Thus, the seed of all human existence is the union of a male (sperm) with a female (egg); its purpose is to unite us; we do so when we return to our original state—when we experience the unending fulfillment of creation.

In other words, kabbalists tell us that the original Light that we spoke about earlier was a positive (male) force that created and united with an infinite receiving force (female) that Kabbalah calls a Vessel. The result was pleasure beyond human comprehension. The sperm and ovum inside a man and woman are the embodiment of the Original Cause, the original Light and Vessel.

To recap, in the beginning there was God, and God created an Infinite Soul which included all the souls of humanity—past, present and future. This is the beginning of all beginnings, the Cause of all Causes. Originally, in this perfect existence of Light and Vessel (God and the One Soul of humanity), *infinite pleasure* was being experienced by the soul through the act of Creation—the union between the Vessel and the Light. This cosmic intercourse takes place every Sabbath!

When two people are in a state of complete happiness and fulfillment, there is zero separation between them. There is only unity. On the Sabbath, total happiness, total unity, total fulfillment is available to us because no curtains separate us from the Lightforce of the Creator. As noted earlier, originally we were born into this exalted, endless existence, but we, the collective soul of humanity, wanted a crack at creating this perfected existence on our own. This is the purpose of the weekdays and the Sabbath. The weekdays give us the opportunity to become our own creator. The Creator gave us the Sabbath to remind us that we will not limp forever. The Sabbath gives us a taste of that perfection so we can go out during the week with complete certainty that perfection is possible for all of us, in every part of our lives.

Creation of the Limited Reality—The Six Days

In the original Perfected Reality, also called The Endless World, the Light was infinite. It was also so intense that one curtain was not enough to dim its radiance. Ten curtains in total were required, one layered upon the other, to convey the illusion of darkness. The last curtain is what finally gave birth to our dark universe including our planet. This can be compared to a beam of light radiating from a flashlight. As the image depicts, a series of curtains gradually diminishes the beam of light until it is practically snuffed out entirely.

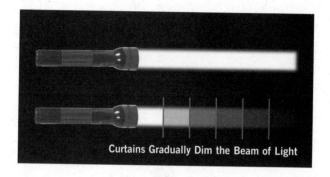

Curtains Gradually Dim the Beam of Light

God did the same thing by fabricating a series of successive curtains, which served, step-by-step, to diminish God's Light. This inevitably produced a reality that is the opposite of the Light.

Kabbalah tells us that the ten curtains created ten different dimensions, and that within each one, a unique realm reflected a specific aspect of the original Light. The first three dimensions—known in Hebrew as *Keter*, *Chochmah*, and *Binah*—are very far away from us. They are known as the Upper Three. Humankind and our universe do not interact or interface with these dimensions. The Lower Seven dimensions are called

Chesed, *Gevurah*, *Tiferet*, *Netzach*, *Hod*, *Yesod*, and *Malchut*; the universe that contains our planet.

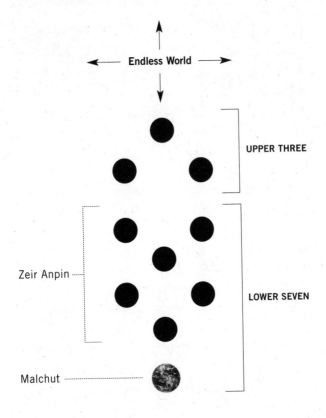

The Structure of the Lower Seven

The Lower Seven dimensions are broken down as follows: six are hidden from humankind (collectively known as *Zeir Anpin*), and the last one (*Malchut*) is home to our physical reality. Our physical 1 Percent Reality is disconnected from the six hidden dimensions, which kabbalists refer to as the 99 Percent Reality or the Realm of Light. When we are connected to it, we draw Light into our lives; we experience happiness, wisdom, and order. When we are disconnected, there is only one word that describes our lives—*chaos!*

During six days of the week the only way we draw the Light of those Six Upper dimensions into our lives is through our work of transformation—all those difficult moments when we resist our self-centered, knee-jerk reactions, and engage in positive actions. But during the Sabbath, the soul ascends effortlessly into these elevated dimensions of Light. No good works are required. From sundown Friday evening until sunset Saturday, our spirit soars into this lofty realm and enjoys free access to the ultimate source of eternal bliss.

The Light we connect to during the Sabbath feeds our souls; it nourishes the very essence of our being so that we have the power to advance our work of becoming the Cause of our own perfection during the week. The Rav always says that without the power and energy of the Sabbath, we wouldn't stand a chance of perfecting our world or changing our lives. The pull of darkness is far too great for us to overcome on our own. But the infusion of Sabbath energy gives us strength, the power to assure our victory over the forces of chaos that reign over this world.

So whatever we are working on in our lives—be it spiritual or physical—if we want to achieve true success, the kind that lasts, we must keep our goals firmly in our consciousness during the Sabbath, the source of authentic transformation. The Sabbath contains bliss and the power to change everything that is not yet bliss.

REMOVING CURTAINS

In the simplest of terms, our purpose in life is to reconnect to the six dimensions that are hidden from us. When we reconnect completely as a result of our own free will, choosing to behave selflessly, we will have created perfection in our world. When we take down the curtains inside our consciousness we allow Light to flow into our lives; now the Light of the Sabbath can shine all the time. A Sabbath that lasts all week, every week, is the ultimate fate of humankind. It's just waiting for us to make it happen.

The curtains of our consciousness are our negative character traits, all those limiting, self-centered qualities that dwell inside us. Our fears, worries, anxieties, bad temper, selfish impulses, insecurities, and envy are nothing more than the absence of the Light of our soul, our true self blocked out by the human ego. However, because we find ourselves in the proverbial looking glass, we search for happiness in the wrong places—we look outside ourselves rather than at the consciousness within. Because society seems to reward aggressive, egocentric behavior we constantly try to outdo the next person instead of extending that person a helping hand. Everything is the mirror image of what it should be.

The world is topsy-turvy. We've got it all wrong, which is the real reason why we age and die. And we have a hard time seeing this because in our mirror image thinking the way things are looks reasonable to us. But they're not. We're going backwards instead of forward. We're dying instead of living. We're warring instead of loving. We're fighting instead of hugging. And all that good, thoughtful, considerate, positive behavior feels uncomfortable to us, instead of feeling easy and right. It seems more natural to criticize and complain than to appreciate and support. But that's all part of the illusion.

Raising Curtains

One thing we know for certain: things in this world are based on the pervasive illusion of change. So if we are not successfully removing curtains, this leaves us with only one option—we're hanging up more curtains. That's right, each time we gossip rather than hold our tongue, or humiliate instead of hug, or steal instead of share, or embezzle instead of give, or scream instead of speaking calmly, another curtain goes up in our lives. The ego grows stronger, and the Light is dimmed. Not only does our life darken, but the rest of the world does, too. All these additional curtains are the Cause of whatever pain, torment, aggravation, chaos, or sadness we might be experiencing.

Six days each week there are nasty obstacles placed before us, but there's a profound reason for this. By putting effort into overcoming these obstacles we transform our inner character, thereby becoming the Cause and creator of our own perfection. Now that you know all your troubles were put there for a purpose, I have one question: What will you do with this knowledge?

Chapter Four

On the Dark Side of the Curtain

BLINDFOLD: THE SIX DAYS OF THE WEEK

From Sunday to Friday we are governed by the physical laws of the universe. Time, space, and motion are part of our everyday existence. Our bodies and our souls are trapped in darkness. Chaos is the norm. We are blind. Even worse, most of us don't even know that we are blind! Enlightenment, at least in its first stage, means finally coming to this realization. The second stage is to remove our blinders completely.

The process of adding curtains or removing them is constantly taking place, whether we know it or not. The process is automatic, invisible, and directly dependent on our every action, including the words we speak. The importance of our behavior is inconceivable as long as we remain in our current state of imperfection. Yet the implications attached to everything we do, large and small, are as tangible and powerful as the unseen force of gravity. If our blindfolds were removed for only a few minutes so that we could glimpse the repercussions of our actions, everyone in the entire world would suddenly run around trying to serve, assist, support and help others unconditionally. Why? We would observe that good deeds pay. And we would see that not only is self-interest a dead end street, but it lies at the heart of all our misfortune.

Each time we react by succumbing to our selfish impulses and desires, we hang up another curtain. If life is as simple as removing curtains in order to unleash an energy force of Light that can create paradise on Earth, then why don't we just do it? Why are we addicted to selfish behavior? Why is caring for our enemy such a difficult task? Why is it so easy to hate, and so difficult to love? Why are we so quick to argue, and so slow to apologize? Why is it so easy to lie and so difficult to tell the truth? Why is it so easy to break promises to others and so difficult to do the right thing?

I focused a little bit earlier on the human ego. Let's discover something more about its origins and its essential nature.

THE CURTAIN HANGER

God also created another entity to challenge us when God fabricated the illusion that we know as this world, so that creating perfection would require a lot of hard work on our part, forcing us to really earn this perfection. (Obviously that part of God's plan is working.) God wove this entity out of the same material as the curtain itself. So we can call this entity the Curtain Hanger. You know this entity quite well, actually, but by another name. Satan.

But Satan, the Curtain Hanger, is not who or what you think he is, based on the stereotype. The word Satan is not just a name; it's a job description. The word means *Adversary or Opponent*. Why Adversary or Opponent? That is the purpose he serves. He opposes us. He challenges us. He tricks us into reacting and receiving. Satan is not a devil. Or a demon. He doesn't wear red. He doesn't carry a pitchfork, and the horns and tail are a myth. He is, in fact, an invisible force that dwells in our minds. He is the human ego.

The sole objective of the Curtain Hanger is to motivate us to hang up more curtains. How? He is constantly coming up with new ways of inciting us to react and to live life selfishly without concern for others. He makes us experience doubt, fear, worry, anger, rage, envy, jealousy and all those other negative feelings in order to justify hurting the other guy. Each time we act on the suggestion of this voice we produce more curtains.

We know the reason Satan exists: we asked the Creator to manufacture an opposing force to challenge us so that we could *earn* the perfection we came here to create. His presence and challenge is what makes our victory feel worthwhile. But Satan has done something to make the game even more difficult. He has concealed himself.

The Blindfold

To keep himself out of sight the Curtain Hanger tore a small strip of curtain and made two blindfolds, which he wraps around our heads. The first blindfold makes us blind to the deeper reality. The second blindfold keeps us from realizing that we are blind. Thanks to this double blindfold the Curtain Hanger is in full control of our lives for six days of the week. (One of his best kept secrets is his own existence!) You see, the Curtain Hanger wants to make it difficult to detect his influence in our minds. He whispers to us, but because we don't see him and often don't believe he even exists, we mistakenly assume his whispers to be our own thoughts. They are not.

Simon Says

As children, most of us played the game of "Simon Says." The person in the role of Simon barks out an order, and the other players do what Simon says if—and only if—the command begins with the phrase *Simon Says*. Guess what? We play Simon Says all day long. Our internal opponent is dishing out all the commands, and we obey like mindless automatons. The Rav taught me a better game to play. It's called *Follow the Leader*. And the leader of this game is your very own soul. When we listen to our souls, we find the Light in every situation.

Ten within Ten

We looked at how there are ten major curtains that serve to diminish the Light of the Creator so that by the time we arrive in our world the spiritual Light is almost completely blocked out. The *Zohar* tells us that each of these ten curtains, or dimensions, themselves contains ten levels. Therefore, to climb out of the lowest level—let's call it level one—you must first climb ten steps. Now you are at level two. Here in level two there are another ten steps to climb. And so on.

Life is all about climbing to higher and higher levels in our quest for perfection. The higher you go, the more happiness you receive in your life. The lower you descend, the more you suffer from depression and turmoil. Make no mistake: if you're not climbing, then you are falling back. If you're not constantly rising then you're tumbling down the steps, level by level. Since everything in this world is based on change, staying where you are is not an option.

Once again, the further you are from the Light the more darkness there is in your life. It's basic spiritual geography. This increased darkness can express itself in many ways—minor or severe financial hardship, illness, marital problems, social problems, crippling fear, anxiety, rotten relationships, and every other known form of chaos. The number of problems in our lives is proportional to the number of curtains we have hung up, which determines our distance from the Light of true reality.

The Weekday Opportunity

Each day of the week is actually an opportunity from the Creator. It's a chance to use the time and space of a single day to remove curtains and draw more light into our lives. We do this by interacting with other people in ways that truly enhance their lives, which in turn allows us to transform ourselves.

One reason it has been so difficult to figure out what life is all about, and thus succeed beyond our wildest dreams, is the structure and energy of the weekday.

Namely, before we can take down a curtain in our lives during the six days of the week, we have to first get by our Opponent—the Curtain Hanger—who does everything in his power to prevent us from ripping down a curtain and drawing more Light in. As noted, our job is to reject him by resisting those selfish impulses that pop into our minds during the week. It's not easy. However, when enough people finally do manage to resist this devious Opponent that's when all the curtains will come down, unleashing a glorious infinite ray of Light that will bathe the entire planet, banishing pain, suffering, and death itself from the landscape of human existence.

What is the threshold? What is that magic number? We don't know. All we do know is that we haven't reached it yet. We have failed to overthrow the ego for thousands of years, so we know this is a tremendously challenging task.

In response to this great difficulty, the Creator gave us a gift. We might go so far as to call it a free ride.

Chapter Five

The Power of the Sabbath

THE SABBATH DAY

For six days of the week, we are stuck on this dark side of the curtain. However, God gave humankind a gift to help us rise to the challenges of these days. This gift is the Sabbath. The energy that is revealed on a single Sabbath is powerful beyond all imagining. If we were to put all the positive actions of a virtuous lifetime on a scale, one solitary Sabbath would weigh far more.

Virtual Reality

We've learned throughout this book that in keeping with the original desire and intent of the human soul, we want to earn Light and perfection. However, during the Sabbath, we are not supposed to engage in any kind of physical work. This apparent contradiction reveals another aspect of the power of the Sabbath. The energy of the Sabbath is *free*. We do not have to work for it. In truth, there is no possible way to work for it, because this Light is of such magnitude that it can never be earned or deserved.

Yes, we work hard, spiritually speaking, to capture the energy of the Sabbath on this special day. But kabbalists teach us that the Light that is our destiny, the happiness that is waiting for us when this game ends, is infinite. Immeasurable. And there is no amount of work that one can perform to merit infinite Light. This is why the Sabbath is a gift. We cannot achieve the ultimate desire of the soul without it, and we cannot earn it on our own.

The inner work we do during the six days of the week, the spiritual effort we exert in our day-to-day lives can only *simulate* the feeling that the Creator wants to impart to us. Life on Earth is meant to operate as a virtual reality game to give us just the *sensation* of earning and of accomplishment. This taste is just enough so that we no longer feel shame when we finally bask in the perfect Light that will delight humankind for all eternity.

So the gift that is the Light of the Sabbath meets us more than halfway here in this virtual reality, helping us to achieve the final objective. If we just allow it in, we are assured of achieving victory. This is the only real work we must do. Let it in. Get out of our own way. Allow the Sabbath to work its magic.

We've just got to get past the Adversary, our egos, which wants us to be slaves to other people's approval, to be controlled by external rewards, and to be an addict to the pleasures generated by forces outside ourselves. Why? This makes us the ultimate Effect, rather than the Cause of our own fulfillment. And that plays squarely into our Opponent's hands.

The Heart of the Matter

The calendar week is much like the human body. The heart nourishes all the organs of the body with blood, keeping them healthy, strong, and functioning at peak performance. The heart of the week is the Sabbath. It pumps Light instead of blood, nourishing the other six days of the week. Lack of circulation in the body causes heart attacks, strokes, tissue death, organ failures, and other life-threatening ailments. Chaos during our week is the spiritual version of bodily disease. Lack of Light during the six days of the week causes chaos in business, in health, and in our relationships with other people.

According to Kabbalah, different forces rule over different parts of the day. Basically, a force called *mercy*, embodied in the rising sun, is awakened at the start of each weekday. And every weekday concludes with the force known as *judgment*, indicated by the setting sun and waning daylight. The Sabbath, however, begins and ends with mercy. We can use this double-dose of mercy on the Sabbath to soften judgments headed our way during the week. Even better, if we capture enough of this Light over the course of the Sabbath, *it* can actually serve to transform the forces of judgment into forces of mercy. Through this benefit alone, the Sabbath offers us value beyond measure.

The End is Now

According to the Bible, the world was created 5768 years ago, as of the writing of this book. Yet science tells us the world is 15 billion years old. Kabbalah agrees with science. Kabbalah described a 15 billion year old universe over two thousand years ago in the book of the *Zohar*. How is it that Kabbalah and the Bible are not in agreement?

The fact is, both estimates are correct. The Bible is referring to the birth of human consciousness, of free will, and of the ability of individual people to contribute toward the transformation of our world into a perfect paradise. That potential is what came into existence some 5768 years ago. So far, it hasn't yet transformed the material world. Kabbalah tells us the world is destined to last six thousand years in its present form. Then the seventh millennium will arrive, ushering in one thousand years of immortality and joy beyond anything the human mind can currently imagine. The seventh millennium contains the birth of the perfect world of Light as described throughout this book.

Here's the good news. The outcome is already settled. The seventh millennium is coming, regardless of what we say or do. And when it comes we are going to live happily ever after. Everyone. All people. Even those souls who left this world over the last few thousand years will come out from behind the curtain that perpetuates the illusion of death. That is the promise made with absolute assurance in the Bible, in the *Zohar*, and by all the kabbalists, including Moses, Jesus, Muhammad, the Prophet Daniel, and the Creator. (By the way, if you are wondering what happens *after* the promised one thousand years of paradise, kabbalists say we will evolve to an even higher level, a realm of happiness so far-reaching and indescribable that kabbalists will not even attempt to discuss it.)

Bottom line, we have no free will concerning our happy ending. It belongs to us. We know this deep in our souls, which is why we crave rest, peace of mind, and contentment right now. We know it's our birthright, our destiny. Our free will concerns choosing the path we take to the final outcome, and even that is not a genuine product of free will. Once again, it's just a simulation.

The TIVO Universe

It's Sunday. The Sabbath is over. Your favorite NFL football team is playing in the biggest, most important game of the season. But your wife has made plans for you to visit her parents—your in-laws. Since you are now a sharing, loving, considerate human being, thanks to the Light you captured on the Sabbath, you happily go along with the plans. But first, you TIVO the game and then you warn your kids that you'll confiscate their iPods if they dare divulge the outcome of the game before you catch it later on that evening.

That night, you grab a diet Coke and then microwave a bowl of nachos and cheese (a contradiction, something you are still working on during the Sabbath) and you sit yourself down in front of your 50" plasma TV. Of course, the game is already over. The outcome is known. Every play, every call, every move, every touchdown has already taken place, but you have no idea what happened. You're clueless (your kids really do love their iPods). And although the game has already been decided, you enjoy every play, every touchdown, every turnover and most of all, the final victory, which is a last-second field goal.

This is life. The outcome is already decided. Every move, every action has already been pre-determined. Every event in your life is recorded on the TIVO player that is your personal existence. Being unaware of the outcome gives you the ability to enjoy the process, and to simulate being the creator and Cause of your fulfillment.

Now here's a secret that modern science confirms, although for some two thousand years it has been considered mysticism to all. The *Zohar* says there are Parallel Universes. That's right, there are two TIVO units out in the cosmos. One of these features a life riddled with chaos. The other features a life where everything is perfect.

We switch back and forth between these two TIVO universes all the time, based on choices we make with our free will. It comes down to this: *to react, or not to react!* Put another way, free will gives us the choice of being selfish or selfless in any given moment. If we react, if we're selfish, we wind up in the chaotic TIVO universe. If we resist that reaction, if we're proactive and selfless then we switch over to the parallel TIVO universe where everything is hunky dory.

Regardless, we are all still heading toward the seventh millennium. If we work hard enough at transformation we may even reach the threshold for world transformation before the seventh millennium shows up. Otherwise, we will continue to bounce back and forth between TIVO worlds until the seventh millennium arrives.

The seven days of our week are a direct reflection of the seven thousand year period. The six days correspond to the six thousand years of transformation, while the seventh day or Sabbath is a direct correlation to the seventh millennium and the Age of Messiah. The opportunity to transform our world and bring the seventh millennium into the here and now is handed to us, week after week.

The seventh millennium is not about time. Remember, time is merely an illusion. The seventh millennium is all about a *threshold of transformation*. Whenever that threshold is met, paradise arrives. The potential is always there. We just need enough people to embrace it. Each week embodies the complete seven thousand year cycle. In other words, through the power of one Sabbath we can achieve the ultimate if we tip the balance past its critical threshold and into eternal euphoric bliss.

The Sabbath and Financial Prosperity

There are three actions that can influence a person's financial state of affairs.

- Tithing
- Spiritual Study
- Connection to the Sabbath

Tithing and study are pretty straightforward concepts. Remember, there are ten dimensions. Our Earth is the tenth, so it represents 10% of true reality. This dimension is under the control of the Adversary, Satan, the Curtain Hanger. When we cut away ten percent of our livelihood by tithing, we are cutting away the Adversary's influence in our lives.

Study and wisdom is all about Light, not the attainment of intellectual knowledge. Thus, the more we study the more change we undergo. The more we change the more blessings we receive, including financial blessings.

According to the kabbalists, a person can participate in the Sabbath and still not reap all its benefits if his or her own consciousness is not in the right place. Therefore, the simple rule of thumb is this: If you do more than you need to during the Sabbath, in terms of effort, preparation and concentration, the energy of the Sabbath returns even larger dividends than it would ordinarily. (This degree of additional effort is relative to our personal means and situation.) The more we break out of our comfort zone, the higher the rate of *interest* we receive from the Light of the Creator.

The Art of Happiness

Kabbalah tells us that the Sabbath is the only time when we can really connect to authentic happiness. The happiness we gain during the six days of the week never lasts; therefore, according to the kabbalistic definition, it is not genuine happiness. Real happiness lasts forever. What we call happiness during the week is really just temporary gratification, provided courtesy of the Curtain Hanger. He has that knack. He can buy us off with a temporary injection of pleasure that tickles our egos, keeping us firmly under his control.

On the Sabbath, however, we have the ability to taste and experience authentic happiness—the kind that lasts forever. During the Sabbath, there is nothing blocking the flow of true happiness. But there is one prerequisite: we must give the Sabbath to someone else. We must find a way to make someone else's day special and filled with Light. The more we become the Cause of someone else's happiness, the greater the flow of true happiness into our own lives.

The Power of Sabbath Study & Prayer Connection

Kabbalists explain that whatever we study during the week, we can't truly take it all in. Why? Because there is an angel who works overtime trying to make us forget the wisdom we acquired. This angel hangs up a curtain and a few days later, we cannot recall the amazing information we thought we'd fully digested. Fortunately, this angel has no jurisdiction during the Sabbath; therefore, on that day, our studies remain firmly planted within our consciousness. The same holds true with prayer. During the week there are many disruptions in the metaphysical communication system between us and the Creator. During the Sabbath those frequencies are wide open.

During the regular work week, our souls capture energy from the realm known as *Binah*.

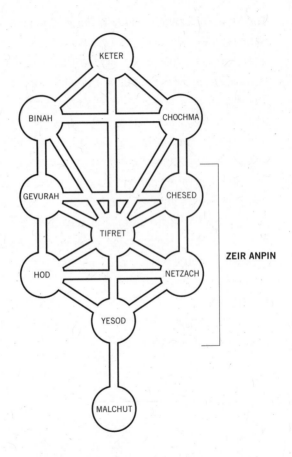

However, the Light emanating from *Binah* must then travel through the six collective dimensions of *Zeir Anpin*. This route has many arteries that can be blocked and disrupted. However, during the Sabbath, the six dimensions of *Zeir Anpin* are bypassed completely and our souls link directly with the realm of *Binah*.

This is why the Sabbath is such a powerful time to launch our prayers. The Creator never says "yes" or "no" to a prayer. The Light of the Creator just *is*. If we just connect to this Force, the Force itself becomes the answer to our prayers. If we cannot connect to it, there is no answer. During the Sabbath, because the obstructions have vanished we can make contact directly with *Binah*, whose Light is the answer to all our prayers. Every one.

The Fires of Hell

Hell is a real place. And it has nothing to do with the notion of punishment. According to the *Zohar*, Hell exists so that negative souls—even those of the wicked—can participate in the paradise, immortality, and joy that is the seventh millennium, the Cosmic Sabbath. Hell is a cleansing process that purifies negative people so they get another chance at paradise. If a person does not transform during his life, lifetime after lifetime, hell is the purification process that literally burns away all the layers of curtains that have accumulated through constant negative, destructive behavior.

The suffering that takes place in Hell is frightening, to say the least, and this book is not the place to delve into it. More relevant is the fact that during the Sabbath the so-called *fires of Hell* are extinguished, since no judgment, not in any dimension, can occur during this unique period of time. Those of us in the physical reality, deserving of judgment, all receive a reprieve during the Sabbath. According to Kabbalah, people who leave this life during the Sabbath also bypass any suffering/cleansing process that takes place in the grave or in Hell. They immediately ascend into the illuminated spiritual dimensions.

In kabbalistic terms there is a difference between suffering and pain. Suffering is a terrible ordeal that serves to purify all negativity, darkness and *curtains* from the essence of an individual. Suffering takes place only because a person refuses to change from selfish to selfless. We are all given many chances to embark on the path of transformation. When we refuse over and over again, when we are consistent in our destructive behavior toward others, the only recourse is suffering, which uproots the ego from the core of our being.

Pain, on the other hand, is part of the technology that prevents suffering, odd as that might sound. Pain is a wake up call that says you are moving in the wrong direction, you have placed your hand on a hot stove, quickly remove it.

The 99 Percent Revealed

The Sabbath is not part of this world—at least not for the soul. Remember, during the other six days of the week, both body and soul are trapped on the dark side of the

Curtain—this world—where we try to take curtains down while the Curtain Hanger tries to put them up.

On the Sabbath day, however, *all* the curtains come down for the soul. The blindfolds come off the soul, too, as it enters into the perfect reality of no time, no space, and no motion. The soul then takes nourishment from this reality, receiving enough Light and energy to encourage it to do its work during the subsequent six days of the week.

Time Travel

Consider the implications of the fact that on the Sabbath our souls gain access to the 99 Percent Realm of Light, which is unencumbered by time and space. Think of the possibilities. Now the soul can travel backwards to reverse disease, illness, decay, and even death itself. The Sabbath suddenly becomes the ultimate source power for healing every conceivable ailment known to humankind—not just physical, but financial, marital, social, emotional, and every other kind you can imagine.

This same infusion of Sabbath energy imbues us with a heightened consciousness so that we can more readily recognize the destructive influences of the Curtain Hanger in our everyday lives. With each new Sabbath connection that we make, our age-old Opponent becomes increasingly exposed. Week by week we develop greater strength, wisdom, and willpower in our struggle against this formidable enemy. Each week we begin to see more. Our doubts begin to vanish. Our skepticism wanes. Our passion for the true treasures of life increases.

The effects of the Sabbath are cumulative. From week to week, an ever-increasing number of curtains are removed from our lives and replaced with a swifter flow of happiness and fulfillment. This is important. Our world will remain fragmented until the dawning of immortality. The only time we can taste that blissful reality—for now—is during the Sabbath, when the soul experiences the Light that is its source. And the Light of the Sabbath accumulates as we move toward permanently merging our dimension with those above. One particular reason the Sabbath is called a *day of*

rest is because our Opponent takes the day off, knowing that on this day we are free of his influence. However, even though we have been temporarily released from the clutches of the Curtain Hanger, we have to use this respite to work extra hard to build a shield for the coming week, so that when he returns it will be that much more difficult for him to penetrate our consciousness. This is the purpose behind the tools given to us by the kabbalists. And this is why, spiritually speaking, in Kabbalah Centres around the world, the Sabbath is the hardest *work day* of the week. Yet, at the same time, it is also the most blissful and euphoric day of the week.

When we talk about technology and tools we are referring to the power that was given to Moses when he stood on Mount Sinai. The story of Moses and Mount Sinai is perhaps the most famous of all biblical narratives, but very few people know what really happened some three thousand, four hundred years ago in history. So let's take a moment to explore the events that took place so long ago on Mount Sinai, for they will shed an even brighter light on the purpose and power of the Sabbath Day.

MOSES AND MOUNT SINAI

The Old Testament (the Torah), the New Testament, and the Quran all offer pretty much the same basic version of the story of Moses, Revelation, and what is referred to as The Ten Commandments. We're told that Moses stood on Mount Sinai as 600,000 Israelites camped at the base of the mountain. God bestowed upon Moses two Tablets. While Moses was receiving the Tablets from God, the Israelites, fearing that Moses had died, built a Golden Calf to worship instead of worshipping the one true God. When Moses returned and saw what the Israelites had done, he dropped the two Tablets containing the Ten Commandments and they shattered into pieces.

This famous story has been part of human culture for thousands of years, yet few really understood what it's actually all about. Only the *Zohar* and the great kabbalists of antiquity got to the bottom of what is unquestionably one of the most mysterious events in all of human history. The first secret the *Zohar* divulges is that there is no such thing as a commandment. In fact, the phrase *Ten Commandments* never appears in the original Hebrew Bible. God does <u>not</u> command, the *Zohar* tells us. God does not reward. God does not punish. Period.

So if God doesn't command, punish, or reward, who does?

The Origins of Judgment and Reward

It is our devious Adversary, the Curtain Hanger, who commands, punishes, and rewards. And he has an accomplice. You. And Me. And all of humankind. Here's how it works. God is simply an endless Divine Energy that imparts happiness, joy, never-ending life and infinite wisdom. God never punishes, nor commands. God does not impose judgment upon us. And certainly does not offer us candy, money, a gold watch, or any other compensation for a job well done.

It is our Opponent who controls the Light in our lives by manipulating us, by tricking us into providing the curtains that we alone fabricate through our own behavior. Let's dig a bit deeper to see how all this works.

The Real Commandment

It is our Adversary who issues commandments—not God. Our Adversary commands us to lose our temper. The Curtain Hanger commands us to scream. Yell. Shout. Cheat. Lie. Worry. Doubt. Panic. React! If we obey, and scream abusively at our spouse, we have just produced a curtain. Voila! The Curtain Hanger has just succeeded in blocking out a measure of Light. Less Light flowing into our lives increases the amount of darkness, which we experience as judgment. Are you following this? It is we who fabricate the curtains that the Opponent employs to impose darkness.

Master Manipulation

Our devious Adversary has a few more tricks up his sleeve. In order to prevent us from catching on to his existence or the dangers associated with nasty, negative, intolerant behavior, the Opponent sometimes actually *takes away* one of the curtains when we behave in a negative fashion. This brings some Light into our lives. See what he's up to? The Curtain Hanger sometimes rewards us for our unkind, sneaky, deceitful or belligerent behavior so that we think it paid off. It gets better. Sometimes when we do perform a thoughtful and sharing action, he reinstates a curtain that he previously removed and our life grows darker. Now we're under the mistaken impression that goodness just doesn't pay.

See the play here?

Satan conjures up the illusion of injustice, lawlessness and random chaos! This is why seemingly smart people do such stupid things in life. They fall for the trap laid by the Curtain Hanger. And still they refuse to believe he exists. It's a brilliant, seemingly unbeatable strategy.

Our Fate is in Our Hands

However, when we wise up to the Curtain Hanger we remove a curtain, and there's nothing he can do about it. *Recognizing* his existence and *resisting* his cajoling is how we triumph and tear down a curtain, letting more Light flow into our lives. It's not God rewarding us. It's our own action. God's Light never stops shining. It's constantly standing by, fully prepared to enrich our lives. We just need to remove the curtain and allow it in. This is how we, as individuals go about creating perfection in the world. The power is in our hands. We just never realized it.

Armed with this understanding we can see the foolishness behind the image of a God who metes out judgment for crimes and misdemeanors. And now we are ready to discover the world's oldest and most important secret.

THE INSIDE SCOOP ON SINAI

What really happened to Moses on Sinai? If it wasn't "Ten Commandments" that Moses received, what was it? The actual phrase used in the original Bible is *Ten Utterances*. The Ten Utterances, according to ancient *Zohar*, are actually the *ten dimensions* that resulted when the ten curtains were initially hung up to block out the Light of the Creator.

So here's what really happened: For many long centuries prior to the revelation on Mount Sinai, the Israelites had been living under the rule of the Opponent. The Israelites and the Curtain Hanger had raised up so many curtains that they threatened to block out every last bit of Light and energy in our world. This would have caused the outright obliteration of humankind. By the time of the events on Mount Sinai, the Israelites were completely ruled by the ego and selfish behavior. They had lost contact with their own true essences. And they had zero awareness of the Opponent who was pulling their strings.

The Secret of Slavery In Egypt

The Bible refers to this completely reactive state of existence as *slavery in Egypt*. Specifically, the Bible says the Israelites were held in bondage as slaves of the Pharaoh for some four hundred years. The *Zohar* tells us this story is code, and warns us not to take it literally.

Cracking the Code

The story is not about a geographical location called Egypt. *Egypt* is a metaphor for the physical world. *Pharaoh* is a code for the Curtain Hanger inside us—our Opponent, which is essentially our reactive, self-centered nature. *The ego is Pharaoh!* This was the slavery that was taking place in the world more than thirty-four centuries ago. On the brink of freedom, the Israelites were also on the verge of disconnecting completely from their own souls, which would have destroyed them and, in turn, the entire world.

Naturally, God was not going to let that happen. So God got involved. Moses was chosen to become the channel for freeing the Israelites from their own internal slavery, which would put the Israelites on equal footing with the Opponent. Moses was sent to prevent the final knockout blow and allow the Israelites to level the playing field. This is what Sinai was all about. The Opponent had the Israelites in a chokehold and Moses, using the technology of Kabbalah, loosened the Opponent's deadly grip, and allowed the Israelites to stand back up and fight once more.

Moses, in effect, disassembled the ten curtains, which allowed the intense Revelation of God's Energy and Light to illuminate our physical world. Now sit down. Open your mind. More importantly, open your heart. Something else happened on Mount Sinai that allowed Moses to break the grip the Opponent had on the Israelites.

Revelation of the Force

When Moses took down all the curtains, in the absence of separators all ten dimensions were now connected as one. This means the Light was free to flow unimpeded, full force, into our world. This intense surge of Light is what broke the Opponent's chokehold. And as a result of this massive infusion of Energy all those wonderful elements that were originally on the other side of the Curtain suddenly became manifest in our world.

A State of Paradise and Immortality

With the removal of all the curtains, death on Earth came to a screeching halt. All humankind experienced immortality. Indescribable bliss infused both the body and soul of every individual upon this planet. It was an exalted level of consciousness beyond all imagining. For the first time in human history, all humankind tasted paradise. Everyone basked in the rush of pleasure associated with *the return of the Endless World.*

A Temporary State

This idyllic, deathless state did not last. Why? Moses had torn down all the curtains on his own; the 600,000 Israelites did not participate in the perfection of the world. *Moses did it for them.* But there was one thing

Moses could not do. He could not defeat the Opponent within each Israelite; they still had to go toe to toe with the Opponent inside each one of them. Sadly, at that moment, not everyone had the internal strength to sacrifice the self-interest that the Opponent had nurtured within them.

The Art of Deception

There were two particular members of the 600,000 who were true masters in the black arts. These two sinister souls were addicted to the energy of the darkness and did not want to see it banished forever. So while Moses was away, these two troublemakers incited the crowd. Using sorcery, they erected a new curtain that conjured up a false vision. The Israelites saw Moses dead, carried off by angels to heaven.

The Free Will Battle

The Israelites had the free will to reject these visions, to show conviction and demonstrate certainty in Moses' promise to deliver them from the slavery of their minds. After all, Moses had assured the Israelites that he would come back down from the mountain, and that the Light of God would free them forever. All the Israelites had to do was practice what Moses had taught them. This is how they could have participated in the arrival of paradise and immortality.

But they did not. They fell in with the illusion that Moses was dead. They listened to their rational minds, not their hearts and souls. They bought in the delusion of death instead of the reality of immortality. Now panic-stricken, they built a physical instrument (think of it as an ancient particle accelerator) that would allow them to connect with the endless pleasure they were so afraid of losing. This instrument was called the Golden Calf.

The Bible tells us that when Moses finally came back down from the mountain and saw what the Israelites had done, he smashed the Two Tablets containing the Ten Commandments. Of course, this too is code. The *Zohar* tells us that the broken Tablets are code for our broken connection to the Light of the Creator.

Fallen Consciousness, Fallen Tablets

As a result of following their intellects and not their hearts, the Israelites lost the freedom of consciousness that Moses had accessed for them. Their fallen state of consciousness is the inner meaning behind the dropping of the Tablets. Suddenly the Light vanished, and a massive curtain went back up as a result of the shattering of the Tablets. Death was reactivated.

Crack Cocaine

Think about it. A person can become addicted to the tremendous high created by just one hit of crack cocaine. So imagine the addiction the Israelites must have been feeling to continuous hits of *endless fulfillment!* And suddenly it vanished. Gone. Not just for the Israelites but for all humankind.

The loss of immortality and endless euphoric pleasure is what leads us to seek out happiness and joy every second of our lives. This is also why we hate pain and fear death so much. *Bliss* is our true origin. *Living forever* is our destiny. And we tasted both on Mount Sinai. That taste, according to Kabbalah, remains imprinted within the DNA and subconscious mind of every human being who has ever walked, or will ever walk, this Earth.

The atoms that made up all the people of the world three thousand, four hundred years ago are exactly the same atoms that combine to create our population today. Perhaps you didn't know this, but atoms never die, according to science. Never. Atoms are immortal. When a person dies, the atoms that made up that person simply circulate back into the environment. Scientists tell us that the atoms that were part of Joan of Arc or Mozart are still present today.

Kabbalah concurs. Except that Kabbalah also says each atom is made up of consciousness, and therefore, the consciousness of Sinai is also present inside each and every human being, which leads to a rather fascinating question—if energy never dissipates, where did this energy force of *immortality* go?

IN SEARCH OF THE ARK

The kabbalists tell us that Moses took the shattered pieces of the Tablets which were still glowing white-hot as a result of the intense energy that radiated through them and placed them in what is known as the Ark of the Covenant. Remember Indiana Jones and the film *Raiders of the Lost Ark*? This Lost Ark is the Vessel into which Moses put the broken Tablets. Not only that, Moses then went back up the mountain where he retrieved a second set of Tablets from God, made of gleaming sapphire, and also placed them together with the original Torah Scroll inside the Ark.

The mind-blowing power inside the Ark is nothing less than the Divine Force of immortality and the absolute redemption of all humankind. This is why the Ark of the Covenant has fascinated us for millennia. Subconsciously, on a soul level, everyone knows that the Ark of the Covenant contains the power to transform this world into a never-ending paradise. Clearly, finding the energy of the original Ark of the Covenant would be the solution to wiping chaos from the face of this Earth.

Locating the Power Source

Now comes the most exciting part of this entire book. Remember how Indiana Jones searched for the famous Ark, racing to beat the Nazis, who were also in hot pursuit? Well, archeologists throughout history and to this very day continue to hunt for the Ark in order to capture the unimaginable power it contains! Governments throughout history have searched for it, too. The Crusades during the Middle Ages were really all about finding the Ark of the Covenant, which was thought to have been buried under the Temple Mount in Jerusalem. Everyone wants to discover the ultimate source of Divine Power! Yet somehow the Ark of the Covenant has successfully remained hidden.

I will now tell you where it is!

The Ark is Found

It shouldn't be surprising, in light of what you've just read, when I tell you that the Ark was hidden behind a curtain. That curtain is in our consciousness and the power of the Ark has been right in front of our noses the entire time. We just didn't see it.

The power of the Ark of the Covenant can be found every week, on the Sabbath. Literally! The Light and energy that was downloaded into the original Ark is released every single Sabbath. How? Every new Torah scroll that is produced and every portable Ark that is built to house and contain a Torah scroll gives us the opportunity to connect to the *original* Ark of the Covenant and the original Tablets on every single Sabbath.

According to the *Zohar*, if an Ark and a Torah are constructed according to the technology of Kabbalah, then they are literally hardwired and networked into the original Ark of the Covenant. This means that the Divine Energy inside the *original* Ark flows through the portable Ark and through the Torah scroll that we created for the Sabbath, releasing a portion of the Light that originally appeared on Mount Sinai! During the Sabbath, we are literally transported back to Mount Sinai and a window of opportunity stands before us: The opportunity to recapture the blissful energy of immortality and true happiness.

You might be wondering why no one has ever found the original Ark of the Covenant. Wouldn't finding the original Ark accomplish the same goal as accessing the Ark and reading the Torah scroll that we utilize during the Sabbath?

Burying the Ark

There's a reason why the original Ark has never been found. There's a reason why there are dozens of theories as to the whereabouts of the Ark but still not a single discovery. It's not meant to be found. Remember the apple seed? Imagine planting a seed for an apple tree. Then, after the tree appears, you try searching for the original seed. It's futile. You won't find it. It's not there. It's invisible. You cannot find the original seed, yet it's everywhere at once.

The original Ark, which contained the Light of immortality, was planted beneath the ground in Jerusalem just like a seed. Instead of producing an apple tree, the Ark produced a *Tree of Life*. Put simply, every single building which contains an Ark and a Torah scroll in our world is another branch of the tree connected to the original seed. The phrase "Tree of Life" is code for the Torah that God gave us so that we can access that incredible, amazing hidden reality.

The Scroll is the Fruit

Every single Ark and Torah scroll (written according to kabbalistic instruction) is like the fruit dangling from the *Tree of Life*.

In other words, when you look inside the Ark and look inside a Torah scroll on the Sabbath you find that original seed, the Divine Energy that illuminated the world during the Sinai event. Now keep in mind, *look*

inside also means to probe the inner secrets of the Torah, which can be accessed through the *Zohar*. To look inside the Torah means to utilize the teachings of Kabbalah to delve into the mysteries of the Torah and master its wisdom, which is precisely what you are doing by reading this book.

Remember, the *Effect always contains the Cause*. The release of the energy of immortality is therefore the ultimate purpose of the Sabbath and the Torah scroll. And this power is not just for Israelites. It belongs to all the world's people.

The Sabbath and the Power of Immortality

When we use the Ark and the Torah every Sabbath, we ignite and unleash these tremendous forces of energy, restoring a portion of the Light that was lost on Sinai. However (and this is a big *however*), as Rav Berg always says, ***knowledge is the connection***. If we do not realize the power that is available to us, the Torah and the Ark are not accessible to us.

A Profound Secret

You might be wondering: will the original Ark remain hidden forever? No. Once the world reaches perfection, the curtains will be permanently removed and the Ark will re-appear as a sign that the transformation is complete. This is why we have never found the original Ark. We have not yet reached perfection. The original Ark comes afterwards not before. So instead of searching for the Ark of the Covenant, we need to search inside ourselves and find those curtains that keep us from perfection.

The Light concealed inside the Ark of the Covenant is already deep inside of us. One candle has the power to light another candle, without diminishing its own flame, and the Light of the Sabbath is a Divine candle that puts fire to the candle already within you and me. The Light of the Sabbath reaches deep within us to rekindle and ignite the Light of Immortality that is the human soul. Our job is simply to connect to the Light of the Sabbath when it comes every week to work its magic.

To bring to fruition these miraculous results, Kabbalah equips us with some powerful technologies, one of which is nothing less than a time-travel device. Remember what we learned earlier about science, molecules and the *time reversibility paradox?* In the realm of molecules, time travels *both* ways, but in our world of the five senses, time seems to only move forward. The Aramaic verses of the *Zohar* operate on the subatomic realm where time reversal is not a problem. Our soul also resides in this realm. Thus, according to the laws of physics, traveling back to Mount Sinai is a perfectly feasible concept.

On the Sabbath, prior to the reading of the Torah, we recite or meditate upon specific Aramaic verses found in the *Zohar*. These words are known as *The Blessing of the Name* (Berich Shemei in Aramaic), and they instantaneously connect us with the consciousness we all reached back on Sinai, thirty-four centuries ago, before the incident of the Golden Calf. Our consciousness literally travels back in time.

To achieve the ultimate goal of immortality (if you are bold enough to embrace it), we must reach a certain threshold of people utilizing the technology of the Sabbath. Then we can tip the scales and completely eradicate the forces of death and darkness from our present-day world. Since the vehicle for this journey is consciousness, we need to begin with our minds, which possess a giant obstacle. You see we don't really believe that the *death of death* is possible. That's the influence of the curtain. It not only conceals what's possible, it makes it difficult to even conceive of such a truth.

It's like being dropped off in a country where everyone speaks a foreign language. Since it makes no sense, the language is meaningless to us. If we never come to understand it, the local language will just become background noise. When it comes to immortality, until we start to believe it and conceive it, we will never achieve it. I know, that sounds like a self-help slogan. But it's not. This is an ancient kabbalistic principle that hovers on the cutting edge between life and death.

The sole purpose of this book is to awaken people to awaken *you* to the wonderful possibility and ultimate inevitability—of a world without suffering and death. This is what the Sabbath has long promised us, but a curtain has concealed this mind-bending truth. Not any longer. This book draws that curtain open. In this lifetime, the secrets of the Sabbath are, at last, being revealed to the masses for the first time in history.

If you're ready to accept the challenge of changing yourself, and in turn, the world around you, the most powerful tool in the history of human civilization stands at your disposal.

If you are inclined to partake in the Sabbath every week just because you did it last week, just because it's part of your routine and lifestyle—stop yourself! Each Sabbath is a brand new opportunity that we receive each and every week. It is the greatest gift humankind has ever been given.

Chapter Six

Activating the Sabbath

THE HEART OF REALITY

At the beginning of this book we talked about the fact that the physical matter around us—including every human being—is merely an illusion. The reality is that we are all made up of one thing: atoms. If someone created a pair of eyeglasses that could only see what lies beneath the illusion, imagine what you would see when you slipped them on. All the people, walls, furniture, buildings, trees, mountains, birds, dogs and cats, cars, and clouds would vanish! All you would perceive is a sea of atoms.

The Substance of an Atom

Since atoms are made up of three particles, the electron, proton, and neutron, you need all three to create the basic atomic raw material of the universe. Kabbalists revealed this two thousand years ago. Specifically, the *Zohar* says there are only three forces that exist when you get to the very heart of reality:

1. A Negative Force (Left Column)
2. A Positive Force (Right Column)
3. A Force of Resistance or Balance
   (Central Column)

Kabbalists explain that we need a structure for our spiritual work, and the Light needs structure in order to be revealed. Just as the atom contains the electron (-), the proton (+), and the neutron, the Vessel, according to the ancient kabbalists, contains a negatively-charged component, known as *Desire to Receive*, a positively charged consciousness that shares, and a third component, resistance, which mediates between the positive and negative forces of consciousness. We also call this mediating force, free will. Incredibly, both science and Kabbalah are describing exactly the same concept! They are just using different words—atom and Vessel—to describe one phenomenon.

THREE PARTS TO THE SABBATH

The Sabbath Day is made up of the same three-column system that is the basis of all of reality, the same three-force model underlying the atom and the electrical current in a light bulb.

On the Sabbath, there is:

- A negative pole, which *attracts* what I call the *God Current*.
- The positive pole, which *radiates* the *God Current*.
- A *filament* that literally operates as a *resistor* in order to illuminate the *God Current* so that Light shines in our life.

On the Sabbath it is our job, as human beings, to activate each of these components in our so-called spiritual light bulb so that we can generate Light. We literally build a spiritual light bulb and then plug it in so that Light shines in our personal lives and in the entire globe.

It may surprise you to know that the key to igniting the raw power of the Sabbath takes place before the day itself. It's found in the preparation process.

The Power of Preparation

Kabbalists tell us that when Moses went up Mount Sinai to connect to the Energy Flow of the Creator, he went on Monday, and then on Tuesday, and again on Wednesday and Thursday. However, on Friday, Moses did not have time to go back up the mountain to connect. Why? He had to prepare himself for the Sabbath. This insight reveals the profound importance of preparation for the energy that is released on the seventh day of the week.

Preparation involves our state of consciousness and some physical preparations as well. First let's deal with consciousness. Part of proper preparation is the understanding that Shabbat gives us amazing power to heal and transform our most negative qualities and actions. So preparation includes a generous portion of penetrating, uncomfortable self-reflection combined with serious appreciation for the power that can remove the Causes and Effects of our negativity. Technologies such as the *mikveh*, preparing certain foods, preparing a table, and candle lighting are all part of the preparation process.

The *Zohar* puts it this way: *Make your Sunday the Sabbath*. The point stated here is that it pays to start preparing on Sunday. And to continue on Monday. And Tuesday. Right up until the moment before the Sabbath kicks in. The act of *preparing* becomes the Vessel that we build, which allows us to hold the Light that manifests on the seventh day. Without preparation, there's no ability to capture the Light. It's as though a deep well suddenly overflowed, unleashing the most miraculous, magical waters on Earth. If we don't have a container we cannot scoop up these magical waters, even though they're all around us. Preparation is your bucket. The actual Sabbath is the day when you can fill that bucket up so that we may drink from this wondrous fountain of youth.

The amount of preparation and hard work that we invest during the week determines how large a bucket we dip into that magical, infinite pool of sacred water. Our quality of life no more and no less is determined by the amount of energy we capture on the Sabbath. And the amount of energy we capture is directly dependent upon the amount of preparation we've made during the six days prior.

It is interesting to note that the kabbalists of history wrote as much about the preparation process for the Sabbath as they did about the mysteries of the actual seventh day itself. That says it all. Throughout history, kabbalists would often stay up all night on Thursday in preparation because there is a particular metaphysical force present in our universe at that time. It is the force known as *Mercy*. Connecting to this force, overcoming the needs of the body through all night study, ensures that there is greater affinity between the individual and the Energy that fills the world on the Sabbath.

The Power of Immersion (The *Mikveh*)

Prior to sundown Friday evening, it is beneficial to immerse in water to remove all spiritual impurities from the body and soul. This ancient practice is called *mivkeh*.

A *mikveh* is a small pool, precisely constructed according to specific kabbalistic instructions. The ancient *Zohar* tells us that the Light of the Creator literally expresses itself in our world as the waters of the Earth. Water is the closest reflection of God's energy in the physical reality. This is why the Earth and a human being are made up primarily of water. The *mikveh* washes away the negative energy we've accumulated over the course of our week so that sparks of Divine Light can begin to shine within us, giving us greater affinity with the Light that will shine during the Sabbath.

Kabbalists explain that we should immerse ourselves in the *mikveh* three times: once to remove negativity; once to remove the *clothes* of the weekday; and once more to draw down the spiritual clothing of the Sabbath

Light. The *mivkeh* brings the soul back to its embryonic state when it was connected to the umbilical cord of its mother, the source of all Light. The *mivkeh* is like the mother's womb, so we are born anew when we exit a *mikveh*.

According to the kabbalists, water possesses the power to truly heal and cleanse us. However, it is vital that we be completely submerged, without even a single hair above water. The negative force called Satan literally sticks on any part of us that is not immersed, and permeates our bodies once again. If one cannot immerse in a true *mikveh*, then dipping in the ocean, a river, or even a pool, if necessary, is a powerful way to prepare oneself to receive the energy of the Sabbath. The more effort we put into immersing ourselves in these ways, the more power we receive.

Getting a haircut, trimming our nails, grooming, putting on clean fresh clothes—preparing for the sole purpose of building our Vessel to receive the Energy of the Sabbath—become profound tools for capturing Light.

It's not the acts themselves, but the consciousness we invest in them that makes the difference.

Washing and grooming is really about cleansing ourselves of the spiritual blockages we've accumulated throughout the week by reacting and by acting in the interest of ourselves alone. Face it: we all react countless times every single day. We allow self-interest to govern our behavior, causing us to be intolerant, hurtful and all-too-often abusive to others. The real problem comes when we do not even recognize this behavior, for then we don't even strive to rise above it. As long as we bring a desire to elevate above our primal, base nature, we are in preparation mode so that we can connect to the awesome forces of the Sabbath.

It's Not About Prayer

Prayer may be the most misunderstood spiritual tool in our possession. Essentially, the notion of prayer, blessings and songs has been completely misconstrued over the centuries. We don't pray to reach God's ear. The provocative kabbalistic insight concerning prayer is that God does not answer prayers. It is we who answer our own prayers by virtue of *connecting* to the power and Force that radiates from God. We make this connection through the technology of Kabbalah and the Sabbath. Do you really think God would say no to a heartfelt prayer? Never. It's sacrilegious to think that an all-loving God would refuse a request for healing from a person afflicted with an illness. Or that God would say "no" to any sincere prayer.

It is we, humankind—you and I—who asked God to create this reality so that we can answer our own prayers and create perfection through our own efforts.

But the Opponent, the good old Curtain Hanger, convinced us to pray instead of connect. What's the difference? Everything! Praying means we are asking someone else (in this case God) to solve our problems; then we passively wait for an answer. As you've probably noticed, the prayers of humankind have pretty much gone unanswered for thousands of years. We've prayed for world peace, the end of pain, and the eradication of poverty, but all of these still endure. Perhaps it's time to make an adjustment. Think about it. After two thousand years of getting no response, might we be doing something wrong? It is we who create perfection; and knowing how to answer our own prayers is what creating perfection is all about!

The answers to all your prayers *already exist!* But they exist on the Light side of the curtain—the other side. The way to receive them is to simply take down the curtain!

The Key to the Lock

Kabbalah's *Sabbath Connection Book* (notice it's not called a *prayer* book) reveals the codes and keys that dismantle the curtains. Another way to understand this *Connection Book* is to know that each word, each letter of a so-called prayer-connection, contributes to constructing the negative-charged pole in our spiritual light bulb. This is what is happening on Friday night. The various words spoken and sung serve as a metaphysical tool that creates the Left Column, the Negative Pole that allows us to capture the flow of positive energy radiating from the Original Source of the Light.

All the various *prayers*, *songs*, and *blessings* are explained in the *Connection Book*. All you have to bring to the game is the consciousness that you are *connecting*, rather than praying. By doing so you are creating a powerful Vessel so that you can draw down the Extra Soul (consciousness) in order to ascend into the Light and capture the additional divine flow of energy that ignites on Saturday Morning and throughout the upcoming Sabbath. To help transform our consciousness, from this point forward I will use the word *connection* instead of *prayer*.

The Power of Hebrew

Sir Isaac Newton learned Hebrew, as did many of the greatest thinkers throughout history. Why? They knew Hebrew was not the exclusive language of one race of people. Like the kabbalists, these great thinkers knew

Hebrew was a universal communication system for connecting to the 99 Percent Reality that lies on the other side of the ten curtains. Each Hebrew letter is like a key or button; combinations of letters are like passwords that grant access to the spiritual world so that Light can flow into our reality. Therefore, all connections made during the Sabbath employ the power of the Hebrew alphabet.

If you were to look at a literal translation of the Hebrew we use on the Sabbath, it would read like a stream of praise, thanks, and other mindless tributes to the Creator—as if an all-powerful God would need such things. A literal translation misses the deeper meaning of these Hebrew words. The power of the Bible and all our prayer-connections is in the Names of God which are encoded in the text's unique sequences. By reading or even just visually scanning these *prayers and meditations*, we transcend their obvious meaning in order to connect to their hidden power.

The Role of Men and Women

Men perform most of the spoken connections on the Sabbath, because male energy corresponds to the Right Column and Positive-charged Pole. The Right Column embodies pure sharing and wholeness, much like the white light of the sun, which contains all the colors of the rainbow. This is why men wear white garments during the Sabbath, reflecting their purity of consciousness and their internal energy of positive sharing. Creating affinity between our consciousness/soul and our actual physical clothing unites the 99 Percent and the 1 Percent within us—the spiritual and the physical.

A woman corresponds to the Left Column and the Negative-charged Pole. Whereas the male represents the spiritual realm and the sun, the woman embodies mother earth and physical existence. The sun emanates rays of light, but it is the earth that is responsible for bringing forth life on Earth. Trees, fruits, grass, all vegetation and all sea life emerge from the womb of the Earth, nourished by the sun. A woman plays the same role in life. She is also responsible for bringing to fruition all the blessings, energy, Light and power released on the Sabbath; this expression of Divine Energy in the physical world takes place during the six days of the week.

Kabbalistically, women are on a higher spiritual level than men (which might explain their heightened sense of intuition, sixth sense, and compassion for others). For this reason, the male performs most of the specific actions related to constructing the spiritual light bulb.

Women participate in other ways. The entire key to the Sabbath begins with the woman. It is by her actions that the entire family (or the individual) connects to the full power of the Sabbath. That action begins with a candle.

The Candle-Lighting

At sundown Friday evening, just prior to the arrival of the Sabbath, a woman lights ten candles, which connect her and her loved ones to the ten dimensions.

This act of lighting the candles seems, on the surface, a simple gesture, but as we know from the *Alice in Wonderland Looking Glass effect,* the simplest of actions is, in fact, the most powerful. The *Zohar* tells us that lighting the Sabbath candles is like turning on a switch that banishes all darkness from this world. Satan, the Curtain Hanger, has a day off on the Sabbath, and it is the physical lighting of the candles that casts him from this physical world. As we learn in Kabbalah, every spiritual event must be triggered by a physical action. In this case the physical action of candle lighting activates the spiritual Light of the Sabbath.

The gentle light of one candle flickering on this side of the curtain is equivalent to five hundred million blazing suns on the other side of the curtain. Now imagine the power of ten candles! How does this happen? Once again, consciousness is the key. Awareness and appreciation for what we receive fires up the inconceivable power of the Sabbath.

There are specific times to light the candles each Friday of every week, which correlate directly to the setting of the sun. A woman should light the candles before the sun has set and the Sabbath has begun. The reason for this is simple.

No Time, Space, or Motion

The Sabbath is a realm of no time, space or motion, in which our souls dwell on the other side of the curtain, the 99 Percent. If on the Sabbath we perform a physical action associated with the Dark Side of the Curtain (our world), our soul is immediately disconnected from the Light Side of the Curtain. This is also why on the Sabbath we do not use electricity, shower with hot water, or engage in other mundane physical activities: if our consciousness is directed to actions associated with a typical day of the week (outside the timeless realm of the Sabbath), our souls are transported out of the Sabbath dimension.

All the bodily restrictions of the Sabbath are designed to locate our consciousness—and therefore our souls—

completely in the realm of true reality, where there is no time, space or motion. For instance, electricity is the motion/movement of electrons via the electrical current, and gas vehicles are propelled by the movement of pistons in the engine. If on the Sabbath we connect ourselves to any kind of motion, like flipping on a light switch or driving a car, our souls disconnect from the realm of the motionless. Therefore, prior to the Sabbath we turn on house lights in rooms where we'll require light and switch off lights in advance where we will not.

Keep in mind this is not an all or nothing proposition. Some people live far away from The Kabbalah Centre in Los Angeles, for example, so they are forced to drive. If we cannot maintain the connection of the Sabbath, it simply means we are not attaining 100% of the power that is available on this day. The more connection we make on the Sabbath, the greater the spiritual wattage we ignite. But it's not all or nothing.

The central idea behind not lighting candles after the Sabbath, not connecting to electricity and restricting other physical activities is really about creating affinity with the still, motionless, infinite Realm of Light that exists on the other side of the curtain. The closer we move toward that realm, the more Light we receive.

The Source of Sabbath Purification

We've learned that the Sabbath can literally produce a brand new body every week—that all of the negative aspects of our body and soul are purified through the power of the Sabbath. One of the ways and reasons this purification takes place is through the presence of Elijah the Prophet at every Sabbath in every time zone throughout the world.

The kabbalists tell us that many millennia ago, the great biblical character known as Pinchas, who was the grandson of Moses' brother Aaron, was so fervent in his desire to preserve the connection with the Light of the Creator throughout the world that he achieved immortality. Both the *Zohar* and Islamic tradition tell us that Pinchas became Elijah the Prophet. Elijah attends every Sabbath connection throughout the world; however, this great immortal soul cannot be present among those who have any sort of negativity or darkness. Thus, the Light of the Creator is forced to purify the entire world just prior to the Sabbath so that Elijah can be present. This purification takes place when women light the candles of the Sabbath prior to sundown.

The candle lighting also helps us to receive children with positive destinies, and increases positive energy and righteousness in our children each week. A woman should give three coins of charity before she lights. Charity—an act of sharing—causes the woman to become a pure Vessel. It is a perfect time to pray for children, for a soul mate, and for peace in the world.

THE SABBATH STRUCTURE

The Negative-Charged Force (-)

Sabbath begins every Friday evening at sundown, and concludes on Saturday evening at sundown. The function of Friday night is to build the negative pole in our light bulb. The kabbalists also call this function *The Building of the Vessel.*

A vessel is a structure designed to receive energy. If you want a glass of water, first you need an empty glass; then you can pour water into it. Friday night is the building of the *empty glass* in preparation for the Divine Water (Light) that will be poured into it over the Sabbath.

The Positive Force (+)

From Saturday morning to early Saturday afternoon our activities serve to assemble the positive pole. The God Current can only be released into our physical world by virtue of the positive pole.

The Filament

Late Saturday afternoon, just before sundown, is the *filament*. Once we build the filament, the full power and Light of the Sabbath ignites in all its splendor. For this reason, late Saturday afternoon is considered to be the highest point of the Sabbath. It is the moment when the energy reaches its highest level and the Light becomes fully manifest.

Here's a quick overview of how we go about building a spiritual light bulb in order to flip on the switch and generate the Light of the Sabbath. Friday we engage in prayer-connections, wine, bread, singing and a whole lot of eating—but for spiritual purposes. The food is literally a conduit for transmitting non-physical energy from the 99 Percent Realm of Light into our physical reality. These activities build up the Left Column, Negative-charged Pole. Saturday morning is the reading of the Torah scroll. The actual recitation of the Torah is what constructs the Right Column and Positive-charged Pole in our metaphysical Light Bulb. Saturday afternoon we engage in what the kabbalists call *The Third Meal*. We break bread and this meal, combined with songs and blessings, assembles the filament so that we now have a complete structure, a perfect Light Bulb. All we need to do is flip on the switch. This is what happens at the Third Meal.

Let's now examine these three components in a bit more detail.

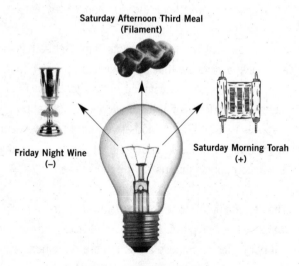

Saturday Afternoon Third Meal (Filament)

Friday Night Wine (–)

Saturday Morning Torah (+)

BUILDING A SPIRITUAL LIGHT BULB

FRIDAY NIGHT:
THE LEFT COLUMN

The various tools that we use come in the form of words, songs and blessings that we recite, which act like building blocks to manufacture the Vessel, the negative pole that connects us to the positive-charged God Current. Kabbalah has another name for this Vessel and negative pole: the *Additional Soul*.

One of the most important aspects of the Sabbath is the additional assistance that we receive to ascend into the Light. Some of this assistance comes to us on Friday night, in the form of the Additional Soul. Kabbalists teach us that in order to house this extra soul we need to expand our Vessel. The material we need for this expansion comes into us during the *mikveh*.

The kabbalistic concept of *like attracts like* and *opposites repel* plays an important role during the Sabbath. Our happiness attracts more happiness from above because these forces are similar. We receive happiness on the Sabbath, and this happiness attracts more happiness, which, in turn, attracts even more.

The Additional Soul that comes to us during the Sabbath is from the part of the soul that existed prior to the building of the Golden Calf, back on Mount Sinai. That soul, which experienced immortality, was in a perfected state of sharing. The human body (otherwise known as the *Desire to Receive*) was also in a perfect state of sharing. Thus there was affinity between the body and soul of humanity and the Light of Immortality. This Additional Soul, available to us during the Sabbath, therefore, helps us—both in body and soul— to ascend into the Light of Immortality because of its similar nature to the Light of the Creator.

On the Sabbath, there is no need to earn our transformation, as we do every other day of the week. This is why the Sabbath is called a gift. The entire world receives this free gift of the Additional Soul on the Sabbath. And it is this gift that prevents the negativity we create through our actions from accumulating to the point of destroying us. Active participation in the Sabbath significantly enhances and strengthens the connection that allows us to capture the greatest amount of Light possible. Simply knowing about the Additional Soul increases its effectiveness during the Sabbath.

Each time we react, hurt someone, or commit any kind of destructive or negative deed, we are physically imprinted with our own negativity; every action of an individual person is written and recorded during all of our many lifetimes on Earth. The Additional Soul received on the Sabbath has the power to cleanse and erase all the negativity that has been imprinted upon us. This cleansing power is activated by the *mikveh* we perform in preparation for the Sabbath.

Receiving the Sabbath

Friday evening begins with a connection called *Kabbalat Shabbat*, which means *Receiving the Sabbath*. We go out, both physically and with our consciousness, to greet this infusion of Light now entering into our world. The physical aspect of "going out" takes place by facing the west. The consciousness aspect is our meditation and thought to be in the Land of Israel, amongst the great kabbalists of history, particularly in the city of Safed, to greet and welcome the energy heading our way.

With our bodies and our consciousness we greet this infusion of Light entering into our world. The aspect of the Light that we are receiving is from the female aspect of the Creator. Thus the ancient kabbalists tell us to awaken within ourselves the consciousness of a groom coming to greet his bride. If we don't recognize this opportunity for connection, it's as though the groom never came to greet his bride.

Part of the Receiving of the Bride technology involves various prayer connections. The great Kabbalist Rav Isaac Luria, who was known as *The Holy Lion* or (*the Ari* in Hebrew), gave us the actual instructions in the *Kitvei Ari* (*Writings of the Ari*), on how to transform ourselves into the groom. This is, without question, the most important technology that we have in our possession. It explains every prayer-connection, blessing, and song that we sing during the Sabbath.

Igniting the Angels (Peace Be Upon You)

After prayer-connections are completed, we sing an ancient song known as *Peace Be Upon You* (or *Shalom Aleichem*). This song connects us to the power of angels, also known as intelligent-energy forces that exert influence in our spiritual reality. The secret behind this connection is found in a Torah story, in which Jacob, the son of the Biblical patriarch Isaac, grandson of Abraham, wrestles with the negative angel related to his brother Esau. Jacob and the angel battle all night long. Finally, in the end, Jacob achieves victory, but first Jacob forces the angel to bless him. Jacob literally forces the negative angel to bring him goodness, converting bad energy into good.

Kabbalah tells us that every Friday night two angels accompany us to our homes. One angel is comprised of positive energy, the other negative. If the energy in our homes is positive overall, then the negative angel is required to bless the home, converting his negative energy into positive. If the home is afflicted with negative energy, the positive angel is forced to *curse* our home, which means the positive energy of the angel automatically is converted into negative energy. Singing *Peace Be Upon You* gives us power over the angels, enabling us to convert all negative forces into positive, even the most negative angel of all, our Adversary, the Curtain Hanger.

The Blessing of the Wine (The *Kiddush*)

The power of the Left Column is embodied in what is known as the *Blessing over the Wine*. This essentially gathers all the Divine Energy that we have accumulated over time and manifests it in physical form. Wine expresses another unique power that we can understand by way of the law of Cause and Effect. In studying Kabbalah we learn that the laws of Cause and Effect govern the world. Furthermore, the Cause is always higher than the Effect by virtue of being first. In other words, the seed is more powerful than the tree, for the seed determines the quality and strength of the final tree. If the seed (Cause) is weak, the tree (Effect) will be weak. If the seed is defective, the fruit will be defective. And if the seed is strong and healthy, the entire tree, from initial root to final fruit, will be strong and healthy.

Wine has the innate power to rise above the law of Cause and Effect. How? A great kabbalist once explained that if you take a grape and squeeze it, crush it, heat it, ferment it and put it in darkness, the result is great wine. This is like us. Only after having gone through the hardships that life places on us can we transform, like a simple grape turning into the finest wine; for as with the wine, to achieve transformation our ego must be squeezed, crushed, and stored in the cellar of our being.

This is one of the few instances where the Effect (wine) is actually higher than the Cause (a grape), which is the reason wine has the ability to draw down tremendous forces of Divine Energy, and induces a high or drunken state. The power of rising above the natural laws of the universe is imbued in us through the power of the wine. With its help we can rise above any negative actions that we have performed in the past (the Cause) because the Effect (us) is now higher than the Cause. This also allows us to avoid any judgments that are coming our way; we can plant a brand new seed for the coming week through the power of the wine.

Correcting the Sin of Adam

The Friday night connection allows us a chance to rectify the original sin of Adam and Eve in the Garden of Eden. Adam and Eve were supposed to wait until Friday night to join together as one. However, they allowed the Serpent (the selfish consciousness within us) to seduce them into joining together earlier. This is why so many of the world's negative actions are related to sexual relations and sexual abuse. The tricky thing is that the intentions of Adam and Eve were good. However, as we all know, intentions are only valuable insofar as they influence our actions. In the case of Adam and Eve, their challenge was to resist the desire to connect too soon, regardless of the circumstances, because resisting impatience and desire is the way to defeat our Adversary.

The Israelites had the same problem when Moses left them to receive the Tablets from God. Their challenge was to resist the illusion that Moses had died and resist the impulse to connect to the Immortality Energy via the Golden Calf. It was not a case of right or wrong, but a case of resisting or not resisting. This happens to us all the time. We react, instead of resisting the impulse to do so. We seek pleasure before resisting a selfish impulse; and by doing so we miss the benefits of sharing that pleasure with others. We react, telling ourselves we are right to do so, instead of realizing that the goal is not to be right, but to resist.

Through the power of Friday night, we are making the connections that Adam and Eve did not; we are elevating sparks of Light that have been concealed since the Original Sin.

Mixing Wine with Water

Red wine, according to Kabbalah, is derived from the negative-charged (-) Left Column energy force, which is why wine has the power to attract energy. So to counterbalance the negative receiving power of wine, the kabbalist adds a drop of water to the bottle of wine as water is derived from the positive-charged (+) Right Column energy force. The Left Column also corresponds to judgment, whereas the Right Column contains the force of mercy. By adding the power of mercy to the Left Column, we literally awaken the force of immortality. To sip the wine after the blessing on Friday night is to sip from the cup of immortality.

The Blessing of Children

After the connection to the wine, parents have the power to infuse their children with Divine Energy, strengthening the connection of each child's body, soul and consciousness to the 99 Percent Reality. The channels of blessings are open on the Sabbath, and the parents are the channels through which the children receive their Light. Therefore, it is important that they bless their children so that the abundance of Light, which is available on Shabbat, flows through them to their children.

The Friday Night Meal and Songs

Physicists and kabbalists both had a problem regarding energy. Physicists solved their problem around the turn of the 20th century. Kabbalists solved their problem more than two thousand years ago. The problem physics had was how to harness the invisible power of electricity in our world. For thousands of years, we lived by candlelight alone. There was no electrical power to light up our homes, to heat and cool us, to power our elevators, street lights, ovens, refrigerators, blow dryers, cell phones, and computers. Then physicists and engineers figured out a way to make the invisible power of electricity a practical force. Without changing the electrical current itself, wires and cables acted as conduits put to use enriching our lives.

The Light of the Creator—the God Current—works exactly the same way. Kabbalists used their own technology to create intermediary devices that allow us to use the God Current any way we want, depending upon our needs and requirements. This is the purpose of the food we eat and the songs we sing on the Sabbath. They are wires. Cables. Tools. Technology. Devices to harness the One Force so that we can Light up, heat up, cool down, and generally transform our lives in the ways that will bring us greater fulfillment.

The kabbalists are clear on this. Without the food, drink, and song, all the effort we put into the Sabbath achieves absolutely nothing. Why? These tools manifest spiritual energy in our physical world so we can use it practically. So start eating, start singing, and Light up your life.

ADDITIONAL SABBATH INSIGHTS FOR FRIDAY NIGHT

The Power of Peace

The great Kabbalist, Rav Isaac Luria, tells us that the Curtain Hanger—our internal Adversary—will try to stir up conflict between people, including husband and wife, prior to the arrival of the Sabbath Friday at sundown. Therefore, this esteemed kabbalist tells us, we must be especially cautious and mindful during these hours. We should make an attempt to counter the Adversary by working to increase the peace between ourselves and our spouses, family, and friends, thus increasing the level of our connection to the Light of the Creator throughout the Sabbath.

Walk with Someone

As the Sabbath approaches, Light is spreading throughout the world, causing negative forces to flee before it. However, as they retreat, they can still inflict harm upon us. If you are out walking on Friday night, it is important to not walk alone. Walking with others—

considered a sharing action—envelops us with protective power.

The Meals of the Sabbath (including Friday night and Saturday lunch)

The Hebrew word for *meal* is *seuda*, which connects to the Hebrew word *sa'ad*, which means to support. One of the purposes of the Sabbath meals is for people to support one another as the intangible Light of the Creator becomes tangible and infused into us through the medium of the meal. Food becomes the conduit to transfer the Energy of the Sabbath. Connecting as a group with the consciousness to truly share strengthens the technology that transmits the Light of the Creator through the food of the meal.

One of the foods eaten on Friday night is fish. The kabbalists tell us that a spark of Light from the soul of a righteous person is always included in the fish. This spark or atom in the fish is elevated by us through the eating of the fish.

All food contains particular Divine sparks of Light, but if we are unaware of this we only capture the physical benefit of the food. When we are conscious of the energy inside the food, we elevate the soul of the animal and the sparks of Light in the food. By doing so, we elevate our own soul and inject more sparks of Light into our world. All these sparks help diminish the darkness.

When people are gathered at a table during a Sabbath meal, another technology for igniting the Light is to share spiritual wisdom with one another. Injecting consciousness, thought, awareness and knowledge into the meal is so important, kabbalists tell us, that without it, life drains out of the moment. On the other hand, in the presence of spiritual wisdom being shared between people, it is as if we were eating a meal in the Holy Temple of Jerusalem.

The singing and good cheer that takes place on Friday night and Saturday lunch is an expression of our happiness that all our negative blockages and karma are being transformed into blessings. The act of singing connects to our inner soul. All of us have a song inside our souls that longs for expression during the Sabbath. By releasing it through singing we bring energy into ourselves and others.

On Friday nights, kabbalists would often stay up until sunrise; or wake up during the middle of the night to connect to the wisdom of the *Zohar*. One of the fondest memories I have of my childhood is midnight study with my father on Friday nights. The Rav and I spent many long years learning sections of the *Zohar* during those quiet hours, and the magic of those moments simply cannot be described. While the rest of the household slept, we'd sit together in the room that served as both den and library, probing the most ancient secrets of the universe, snacking on nuts and other goodies. It was a true taste of heaven for me.

The idea here is for all of us to go the extra mile on the Sabbath, putting forth an effort that is out of the ordinary, like getting up at 3:00 AM to invest some time to learn. When we rise above our nature, miracles take place in our lives.

SATURDAY MORNING: THE RIGHT COLUMN

The most powerful start to Saturday morning, for a kabbalist, is another *mikveh*. It prepares us for the second aspect of the Additional Soul that is being infused within us. The part of the soul that comes to us now is completely different from the part of the soul that arrived on Friday Night. The second *mikveh* helps us change our consciousness so that we are also different people on Saturday morning. The *mikveh* in preparation for Friday night was about removing negative influences (Satan) from our being. The *mikveh* on Saturday morning is about receiving the spiritual Light and allowing its influence to enter our world.

The Light we connect to is the male part of the Creator. This Light supports the power and technology that we receive from the Torah scroll. The Light available to us on the Sabbath is not something that we can contain in our weekly Vessel. The Additional Soul that we receive throughout the Sabbath helps us to contain all the Light we receive on the Sabbath.

The Torah reading on Saturday morning is the instrument we utilize to ignite the Light that emanates from the 99 Percent, the male aspect of the Creator. The Torah, the Positive Pole, is activated by virtue of reading. Participants in the Sabbath need only to listen and hear the reading to make the connection to the Torah and thus build the Right Column, Positive Pole within their own consciousness.

The Torah readings were originally structured by kabbalists thousands of years ago to coincide with the fifty-two weeks of the year and to correlate to the various cosmic influences that become available each week. Some weeks we access the power of healing. Other weeks we derive the strength to banish doubt and uncertainty from our consciousness. There are countless forces that can transform our consciousness each week. The way to access these various forces and benefits is to know and understand what is actually available.

If the Torah is used as a weapon of war against the ego, specifically, to wipe out all self-interest from our own consciousness, then the Torah becomes the *Tree of Life*, a connection to the 99 Percent Reality of the Light. On the other hand, if you are listening to the Torah merely out of tradition, or religious devotion, then in the view of the *Zohar* and the great kabbalists of history, the energy derived from the Torah will be nil. And according to the renowned 20th century Kabbalist Rav Yehuda Ashlag, if the Torah is used for self-centered purposes, such as honor, praise, and self-righteousness, then the Torah becomes "the drug of death."

So although the Torah is the ultimate instrument to restore the forces of immortality that were present on Mount Sinai, it can also be a highly dangerous and destructive force if we misuse it. The Sabbath is a serious business and what we do on this day can do us great harm or great good. The choice is up to us.

The Names of God

The purpose of the Torah reading is not simply to recount biblical stories that took place many thousands of years ago. The stories are code, external garments that deftly conceal the incredible power that radiates through the Torah's ink and parchment. Specifically, encoded into the words, sentences and verses of the Torah are *Names of God* that activate particular forces of energy. Kabbalists tell us that by listening to the words of the Torah read aloud, those specific vibrations are picked up by the eardrum and reverberate directly into our soul. It's not the literal words, but the Names of God that are encoded into the vibrations of each word that have this extraordinary effect.

The kabbalists of history, notably Kabbalist Rav Isaac Luria (the Ari), identified those Names of God so that we can strengthen our connection to them when they appear.

The War Room

The Rav was acutely aware of the seriousness and dangers of misusing the gift of the Sabbath. Prior to the Rav meeting his Kabbalistic Master, Rav Yehuda Brandwein in 1962, the Rav was part of the mainstream orthodox community. The synagogue on the Sabbath, in most traditional synagogues all over the world, usually featured many business discussions commemorating the past and other activities that were motivated by self-interest instead of internal spiritual warfare. The Torah reading was usually fast with the intent to get it over with as soon as possible.

For this reason, the Rav refused to call the area in The Kabbalah Centres where the Torah reading takes place, a synagogue. Instead, it is called the War Room!

We are there to receive the energy to wage war against the Curtain Hanger, our internal Opponent who is the cause of all our misfortune. That is not to say that people who participate in a Kabbalistic Sabbath do not have jealousy. They do. I do. All of us possess the same negative traits because all of us receive the same negative impulses and thoughts from the same source—the Opponent.

The only difference is that we admit it. We recognize the source of our ill will, envy and complaints. The difference is we are there to fight it. If this kind of consciousness permeates the War Room during the Torah reading, then the forces of immortality are released into the world and we move one step closer to banishing all the curtains separating our world from true paradise.

Seven Torah Readings

During the Torah reading, seven different men are called to the Torah to act as channels to connect to the specific energy relating to each one of the Lower Seven dimensions (seven *Sefirot*) that connect with our universe. Each person helps to connect us to an entire dimension. The final person takes all the energy that has been aroused and serves as the channel to manifest it into our physical reality, thereby completing the energy necessary for the construction of our spiritual Light bulb.

One Single Goal

There should be but one goal on the mind of each participant during the Sabbath Torah reading—the removal of the curtains inside of us (our negative traits) so that we may restore the Light that we tasted on Mount Sinai. The goal is total perfection, fulfillment, and immortality. To settle for less is to deny the power that God instilled in the Sabbath. To aim for less is to accept the curtains inside us that prevent us from seeing and feeling the true purpose of the Sabbath. To accept less is to allow death to continue its rampage, and to prolong the arrival of our Final Redemption.

Changing Names and Naming Babies

Kabbalistically, a person's name is connected to his or her spiritual DNA. For this reason, during the Sabbath and the Torah reading, there is a particular moment when we can change a person's name to alter his or her destiny and help this individual achieve personal transformation. The purpose and power of a name is found in the Hebrew word for soul, which is *Neshemah*. In the root of this word (*NESHEMAH*) we find another Hebrew word, which is *SHEM* or NAME.

When kabbalists give someone a new name, this is his or her *Soul* name. That person's English name (or name in whatever one's native language may be) remains the same.

The complete soul of a baby does not materialize until the Sabbath. When the newborn child is female, during the Sabbath there is a baby naming for the child. This takes place after the child has experienced one complete Sabbath without a name so that her complete soul is infused into her body.

A kabbalist will never name a child after a dead or even living relative because the emotional, spiritual and physical baggage of that person will be transferred to the child through the name. According to Kabbalah, we inherit the karma of the person after whom we are named. This is the underlying reason why kabbalists name children after the great men and women of the Bible.

Therefore, names are chosen from among the great biblical figures in the Torah not because of tradition, but because the letters of the alphabet that compose a specific name in the Torah possess the precise *genetic* qualities that empower the person. These qualities are passed on to the person who acquires the name so that he or she can achieve one's own spiritual transformation and greatness during the course of one's own life.

Healing

On the Sabbath, the Light of Healing becomes accessible. Specifically, after the sixth Torah reading we can access this Light for ourselves and the world. At this time we meditate upon one of the Names of God known by the three Hebrew letters *Mem*, *Hei*, *Shin* מ.ה.ש. This particular sequence ignites healing energy. These same letters, rearranged, spell the name

Moses, (*Moshe – Mem, Shin, Hei*) who was the first true divine healer.

When Moses' sister, Miriam, contracted leprosy, Moses healed her using the kabbalistic healing incantation, *El, Na Refa Na, La*(God, Please Heal Her, Please.) Just as Moses transformed the judgment of Miriam's disease into the force of mercy, we can use the energy of the Sabbath, which is pure mercy, in combination with the re-sequenced name of Moses—*Mem, Hei, Shin*—to gain the power to heal.

The most important thing we can do during this special moment on the Sabbath is to meditate upon anyone who needs healing, thinking about this person's name and their mother's name in order to penetrate to the person's soul at the level of its DNA. By taking care of another in this way we activate the Light of healing to fill our being and those that need it most.

SATURDAY AFTERNOON:
THE CENTRAL COLUMN

Saturday afternoon, specifically the Third Meal, is the construction and assembly of the filament. This is the climax, the highest point of the Sabbath, the moment when we capture all of the Light we might have missed in our earlier Shabbat connections. When the Sabbath began, we were working to remove fragmentation from our lives and this world. By the time we reach the Third Meal of the Sabbath, we are achieving perfect oneness.

The great kabbalists tell us that the Final Redemption of humankind is intimately connected to the Third Meal of the Sabbath. It is here, at this precise moment, that we determine *how* and *when* the Redemption will take place. The Final Redemption refers to the time that death will actually come to an end. This will coincide with the arrival of the Messiah. However, the kabbalists tell us that the Messiah is not coming to save us. Rather, the arrival of the Messiah is a seal that confirms that paradise is now upon us. It is we—you and I—who determine when this Final Redemption will take place. That's in our hands. It always has been. But the Curtain Hanger has deceived us into waiting passively for the world to change instead of taking control over our lives and using the God-given gift of the Sabbath to hasten the arrival of a peaceful world where death no longer exists.

Make no mistake: Our final fate is already sealed. The outcome is pre-determined. All humankind will participate in paradise. Our story has a happy ending. We will all live happily ever after, even though the curtain often makes it hard for us to believe that. Death is an illusion. This world is an illusion. Our departed loved ones all dwell in a reality far more authentic than this, and when the Final Redemption takes place they will return to this reality with all the other souls of history. I know, I know, this one is hard to fathom. But the kabbalists tell us that this world—this life—is more like a dream, and when it finally comes to an end, when death is finally over, we will wake up to a new, far more elevated consciousness.

While we're still in the dream, the pain feels real. It hurts. But we can choose how quickly we ignite our redemption. This is the beauty of free will. It is up to us to decide how quickly we take down the curtains and achieve perfection. The longer it takes, the more painful the dream will become.

Thus the Sabbath is really about building a powerful movement of committed people. The more people who participate with the shared consciousness and shared goal of truly ending chaos, the more quickly we will bring about the permanent end of all suffering and death.

The Central Column

According to Kabbalah, the increased suffering that can take place as a result of delaying our Redemption is connected directly to the immune system. Armageddon is not about nuclear holocaust or an asteroid that destroys all life on Earth. It is the destruction of our immune systems that will pose the most serious threat to our world. This danger is aggravated by pollution, and by global warming. And if our immune systems aren't strong, perhaps it will be a virus that decimates our numbers. Remember, at various times in history it is the viruses and bacteria that have caused the deaths of millions of people at a time. Today, in our highly interconnected world, in quite a short time a single virus or bacteria could destroy billions of us.

The power and the promise of the Third Meal energy on the Sabbath is about strengthening our immune system and that of the Earth so that this frightening scenario never takes place. Participating in this seemingly simple weekly spiritual event is powerful beyond all imagining. If we could actually see the magnitude of spiritual energy being awakened at this time, it would literally take our breath away. People would be lined up for miles trying to get into the Sabbath's Third Meal. However, thanks to the curtain, the Third Meal of the Sabbath has been the most neglected part of this transformative day.

The ancient kabbalists tell us that those who participate regularly in the Sabbath, especially the Third Meal, with full consciousness, will be protected and blessed even during times of great chaos. However, our goal is to employ the power and energy of the Sabbath and the Third Meal to ensure that *all* chaos is removed from this world. Our goal is to bring perfection to all humankind, and ensure that the Final Redemption takes place swiftly and smoothly, without all the fire and brimstone of the doomsday prophets. The only fire and brimstone we need is the kind that wipes out our ego. The only bomb that needs to be dropped is the one that lands on the ego. And that bomb is made of pure Light and is available every Sabbath—most especially during the Third Meal, when the Light Bulb actually goes on.

The Filament

The Third Meal serves the same function as the filament in the light bulb. The filament—the third component—mediating between the positive and negative poles, is the piece of the puzzle that allows us to manifest the Light that is otherwise just potential. It is the filament that glows and emits Light as it creates resistance. Similarly, the Third Meal is one of the most powerful tools to help us resist the voice of our Opponent. The more we resist our own Opponent within, acting like a filament, the more Light shines in our lives. During the Third Meal, the Earth, our 1 Percent Reality, has connected to the 99 Percent. The God Current is flowing. Light is the result.

Construction
Friday Night and Saturday Morning we construct the Spiritual Light Bulb

Connection
Saturday Afternoon we connect the Bulb and receive our infusion of Light that lasts for the entire coming week

The Desire of all Desires

We learned throughout this book that we need a Vessel in order to attract and contain the Light of the Creator. A Vessel is simply the desire that burns within our consciousness. If we have a desire, we attract energy. Period. However, selfish desires only attract a temporary flow of Light, so happiness derived from selfish desires and actions do not last.

Kabbalistically, selfish desires therefore make weak Vessels. Desires for genuine Light for the *Sake of Sharing* with others are powerful Vessels; they ensure a constant flow of energy through us, the channels, to other people. Such desires are a shrewd play on our part because we derive all the benefits from that Light as it flows through us. In other words, if we need healing, we should never desire healing for ourselves. We should meditate to use the Sabbath energy to send healing to others. Why? The Light that channels through us, en route to other people, automatically heals us as it passes through. Likewise, if we send the Light of financial prosperity to other people during the course of our prayers, that Light will ignite prosperity in our lives. That's the beauty of a technology that benefits every life it touches.

If we desire peace in the world, healing for all who need it, and unending happiness, especially for our enemies, all that peace, healing and happiness flows through our lives as well. If our desire is for personal perfection of our soul, to fulfill the original purpose of our individual creations, we will receive the Light of the Creator as that perfection is achieved.

This brings us to a secret: the harder it is for us to share with others, the more Light we reveal. The more we resist our selfish nature and truly care for others, the more power we get in our lives. Praying for our enemies is probably the most difficult thing for us to do (the ego hates enemies). However, it creates the ultimate win-win because when we bring our enemies happiness they no longer will feel animosity towards us—or toward anyone. Why would they, if they are happy? And it brings us happiness because the Light must flow through us first.

The problem is our Adversary and ego. It will do everything in its power to make us pray for ourselves alone. The ego is all about receiving. Receiving is a small desire. The greatest and largest of all desires is the pure, absolute, complete *Desire to Share* with the world. This kind of perfect, unselfish desire brings us everything we desire. Our problem is that our desires are small when it comes to praying for the welfare of others, most especially our enemies. And this is why we lack unending happiness and good fortune in our own lives. Our desires are tiny.

The Third Meal offers us an opportunity to ignite the *Desire of all Desires*. This means that once we reach the point where our *Desire to Share* is unlimited and truly genuine, we will receive unlimited Light and blessings forever. When a critical mass of people attains this level, it will mean immortality for the entire world.

How do you know if your *Desire to Share* with another is genuine? You will know if, at first, you are afraid to pray for others because you are afraid that you will receive nothing. That fear is a curtain. If you overcome the fear and pray for others anyway, you have torn down a curtain. In order to activate a prayer for another, it must be a pure desire. Unconditional. And if it is, then the Light flows through you. In other words, the more you choose not to receive the more you will receive.

This kind of true desire is difficult to achieve. This is why we have the Third Meal. It infuses us with the desire, without an agenda, to ask for the Light for the sake of others. And if we do not have a desire to have a desire then we can ask for that as well, and attain a desire to have a pure desire.

It should be coming clear to us that Third Meal is the greatest opportunity in the world to affect genuine peace and immortality.

Personal Wish

During this unique moment of the Sabbath, the cosmic gates to the 99 Percent World of the Light are wide open. This is the perfect time to make a personal wish. As we've seen the best possible use of this opportunity is to make a spiritual wish, a wish for personal transformation that supports others and the world.

SEPARATION AND SAFE LANDING (*HAVDALAH*)

At sundown Saturday evening, the Sabbath comes to an end. Throughout the Sabbath, our soul has elevated to the highest levels of the spiritual worlds. We do not want a sudden crash landing. To avoid that, the kabbalists instituted a technology that ensures a safe and soft touchdown. It is called *Havdalah*, which in English means *separation*.

Now our goal is to safely separate ourselves from the stratospheric spiritual realm that we visited during the Sabbath. Using wine, a myrtle branch, and a special candle, we recite a few kabbalistic meditations, which act as an autopilot to ensure that we enjoy a comfortable return.

It is said that all those who smile and laugh during this connection arouse the forces of financial sustenance.

When we connect to the sweet aroma of the leaves of the myrtle branch, the additional soul leaves. The instant it does, Satan is back. For this reason, we often experience confusion and find it easy to lose our temper Saturday evening as the Curtain Hanger works overtime to regain a foothold in our lives. As this time is the metaphysical seed for the coming week, it is especially important to maintain a positive consciousness and not react to the chaos.

Escorting the Queen (*Melava Malka*)

King David was destined to live for a short time on Earth and die on the Sabbath. However, Adam foresaw this so he gave King David seventy years from his own life so that David could accomplish all that he was meant to accomplish spiritually in this world. At the conclusion of every single Sabbath, an unimaginably appreciative King David would sing praises and offer thanks to God and to Adam for giving him the gift of life.

This gift of life is connected to the energy of immortality. Kabbalists love immortality. Thus, every Saturday night, we re-enact King David's actions, employing the same technology he used. It is called the Fourth Meal, or The Meal of King David, also known as *Escorting the Queen*. The Queen is the Light we experienced on the Sabbath and now we are escorting Her out of our dimension as She returns to the 99 Percent Reality.

When Adam and Eve were first created, they were immortal. After eating from the Tree of Knowledge, their *Desire to Receive* created separation between them and the 99 Percent Reality. Death was born. Kabbalah tells us that there was one part of the body of Adam and Eve that was never nourished from the Tree of Knowledge, and therefore does not know death. It is called the *Luz* bone and it is found at the base of the skull. The Luz bone is immortal. Both Israelites and Muslims maintain the same view of the Luz bone. The prophet Muhammad said a special rain will come at the End of Days that will activate this bone and bring about resurrection. The kabbalists say virtually the same thing, referring to dew that will fall and ignite the resurrection through this unique bone.

Rav Yehoshuya ben Chanarya in his commentary on the Torah said the following about the Luz bone:

> "He put it in water but it did not disappear, he ground it in a mill but it was not destroyed, he put it in a flame but it was not burned, he put it on an anvil and began to pound on it with a hammer. The anvil broke and the hammer was split, but nothing harmed the bone."

The kabbalists tell us the Luz bone is not nourished during the week but only during this Fourth Meal; *only* the Luz Bone is nourished at this time.

Consequently, the Light that is being released through the food is obviously from the Tree of Life, the energy of immortality. Therefore, whoever participates in this meal connects to immortality and the power of the Resurrection of the Dead.

Chapter Seven
Achieving Immortality

The Details of the Sabbath

There are many insights and details pertaining to the various activities we perform during the Sabbath—from Friday sundown all the way to Saturday sundown. I would need a dozen separate volumes to convey the full technology of the Sabbath to the reader. But the basic consciousness one should have is that the Sabbath is about connection, not prayer or tradition. It's about restoring the forces of immortality that were lost on Mount Sinai three thousand, four hundred years ago. It's about tapping into the original Ark of Covenant and the original Torah scroll and Tablets contained within it. The Ark and its powerful contents are the wellspring and fountainhead from which this Divine Power radiates.

There is no other reason for the Sabbath's existence. It's not about coming to a place of worship to hear inspiring words. It's not about remembering the past or self-reflection. It's about ending death. It's about infusing the world with the Light that Moses originally brought into the world. To expect and demand anything

less is to deny the greatest gift God gave humankind—
the ability to participate in bringing about the perfection of the world and ending the reign of death forever.

The Purpose—Plain and Simple

When we reach a critical mass of people using the Sabbath to pour Light into our world, a threshold will be reached where Light overpowers darkness and we achieve forever the perfected state of joy and immortality that all humankind experienced momentarily at Mount Sinai. To go to a synagogue each week to *pray* as an act of tradition; to carry on the heritage of our fathers and forefathers while the world continues to burn and bleed is an exercise in futility, and is a terrible waste of the power that is given to humankind every Sabbath.

Similarly, to treat the Sabbath as an opportunity to escape the chaos of life and socialize up with good friends, or to center ourselves after a hard week, is a nice thought, but a tragic missed opportunity. If you need to time to ground yourself and escape the chaos of life, take time off during the week for an hour or two and meditate or go for a walk. The Sabbath is a time to inject into the universe (and your life) nothing less than the power to eradicate death.

Defining Death

Make no mistake: the force known as *death* is an actual external form of energy that infiltrates our lives. The death force is the underlying culprit behind all chaos. For instance, when we're sad it means our state of happiness has died; death has somehow entered our life and killed off our happiness. When we're bored, fearful, angry, or depressed, it's not some external situation or person that is ultimately responsible. This person or situation is only the Effect not the Cause. The real Cause is the death force, which was able to penetrate our lives. All chaos, every bit of it, is caused by the death force. Every tiny bit of turmoil, all aggravation and pain, large and small, occurs because a certain measure of the death force came into our lives and killed off our happiness and serenity.

The death force is not an absence of Light. It is an actual entity that feeds and lives off of the power that we give it. The reason we finally die is because our negative actions have caused an accumulation of death energy. Here's one more secret concerning the force of death. You might have heard about the so-called Angel of Death. Well, guess what? The ancient *Zohar* tells us that the Curtain Hanger, our Opponent within, *is* the Angel of Death. The Opponent and the Angel of Death are *not* two separate entities. They are one. And the force inside you that impels you to react in anger and do all the negative things that you don't really want to do, that *voice of persuasion* is the Angel of Death himself.

Since we know that our egos are really the Opponents, therefore it is our ego who is the true, unseen Angel of Death. The ego incites us to react to its every whim. And then it hangs up a curtain creating chaos in our lives, which allows it to grow stronger. When we allow our egos, our Opponents, to acquire so much power, we inevitably die because of all the darkness and death energy that accumulates inside us. Whether it's a car accident, cancer, heart attack, stroke, AIDS, or even suicide, the underlying culprit is our internal Opponent. How the Angel of Death executes the chaos that causes death is secondary. Those are merely the Effects, not the Cause! And the doubts you're having about all of this right now are caused by the curtain inside your mind that blinds you from seeing and feeling this powerful truth.

The True Power of the Sabbath

The unveiling of the true Angel of Death will now help us to further grasp the power that the Sabbath offers us. When Moses stood on Mount Sinai, all the curtains were removed and the blazing Light of the Creator banished all darkness, even the Angel of Death. But as we learned, because the Israelites didn't conquer their own Opponents, the condition of immortality and the state of infinite happiness that ignited on Mount Sinai could not be sustained. And so the Light was lost. All of this power was then concealed and stored inside the Ark, which acts as a reservoir so we can tap into it every week and gradually repair the damage. Each week we have the chance to wipe out the Opponent, tear down the curtains and reestablish paradise on Earth. It is the Sabbath, the proverbial Day of Rest, which gives us nothing less than the ability to turn the tables on the Angel of Death, the dreaded Curtain Hanger, and end his existence once and for all.

This is why the Curtain Hanger used his powerful influence throughout the ages to corrupt the meaning, purpose and power of the Sabbath. Incredibly, people have been going to synagogues, churches, and mosques for hundreds of years, yet the chaos and suffering in the world has remained virtually unchanged. We have been duped by the greatest fraud and deception ever perpetrated against the human race; *religion!*

Kabbalah and the Sabbath are not about religion. The Sabbath and the technology given to Moses were designed to help us wage the war *within*. This is a technology that helps eradicate the curtains inside us so that we can connect to the Divine Realm of the 99 Percent.

If an individual truly removed his or her inner curtains and achieved one's own perfected state of existence, that individual would have no reason to hate, argue, fight or even disagree with anyone on Earth. The only reason we ever fight with someone else is that we feel a deep lack within ourselves. We want something, and we believe that the other person has it. If, however, we were truly filled with everything our heart desired, there would be no reason to cast a jealous eye on the possessions of another.

The Sabbath can give each person everything that person wants out of life. And because the Light is infinite, everything you receive in no way diminishes what the next person receives. There is enough happiness to go around for everyone. And infinitely more beyond that. But it's hidden behind the curtain, just waiting for us to discover it.

Life is not complicated. The Light of happiness is everywhere. God is everywhere. Make no mistake. The answers to our prayers are everywhere. Without question. So what's the problem?

The curtain.

Remove the curtain and the personal pain is over.
And global pain will end just as fast.

The Real You

Our true nature, deep inside, behind the curtain, is one of unconditional sharing and unconditional love for our fellow man and woman. I know, it's hard to believe. But at the level of the soul the Jew really, truly loves the Muslim and the Christian with all his or her heart. And the Muslim really loves the Christian and the Jew with his or her entire being, deep inside. And the true Christian cares deeply for the wellbeing of the Muslim and the Jew.

The hatred and discomfort we feel toward those different from us is caused by the curtain. Through illusion it leaves us in a reality where everything is the opposite of the way it appears. It creates an upside-down state of mind. Therefore, the greatest hatred can really be transformed into the greatest possible love—when the curtain comes down!

However, for now, we live on the dark side of the curtain and the opposite state of unconditional is conditional. Therefore, in the illusion that is our physical reality, our natural tendency is to set conditions on everything we do. Every action that we take, no matter how selfish, neutral or altruistic it may appear to be, always has a hidden agenda.

Because of the curtain in our consciousness we cannot even fathom the tremendous benefit that accrues from unconditional friendship and total care for another human being. Every bone in our body is ruled by self-interest; is governed by the survival instinct—courtesy of a powerful illusion. Only when we tear down the curtain does our true self, our soul, come shining through. Only when we catch a glimpse of what lies behind the curtain do we recognize the power of sharing, and see what life is really all about: by giving first we receive everything we need in life to achieve true happiness and unending life.

It's About Re-Creating Perfection

Never forget: it is by design that we are completely out of touch with our true selves. We are born into this world on the dark side of the curtain of consciousness. However, as we take down the curtains our true self comes to light. As it does, we begin to feel indescribable fulfillment. But as long as those curtains remain up, we will never, ever be convinced that making someone else's life happy is the way to bring about immortality for all humankind and for ourselves!

The Bottom Line

The Sabbath is all about removing curtains so that we can master *Love Your Neighbor as Yourself*. Not for moral reasons. Not because some religion tells us to.

But because sharing will inevitably remove the scourge of death from our world. The only hurdle we must overcome each week on the Sabbath is doubt. This curtain is what causes us to doubt the fact that death is an illusion, and immortality is our destiny.

The good news is that the Sabbath connection, performed properly, removes our doubts. The Sabbath connection, experienced with the right consciousness, offers us the power to believe, conceive, and achieve anything in our lives, including the removal of all doubt and skepticism.

The Sabbath is a gift from God that serves one singular purpose: to restore the state of immortality and indescribable joy that existed on Mount Sinai. That's it, plain and simple. The Sabbath is about making the entire week one long, eternal Sabbath where the only reality is simple unending delight and eternal existence.

Then the nightmare that we now find ourselves in—our chaotic world, will finally end. Forever. The reality of immortality will become manifest. And it will remain so forever.

No longer will the Sabbath be a single Day of Rest. It will be unimaginable happiness for everyone, for all eternity.

It's a perfect ending. And it's a perfect new beginning.

Prolonging the Light

Throughout history, every Saturday evening when the Sabbath ended, kabbalists would wish one another—and their students—a heartfelt *Shabbat Shalom* (Peace on the Sabbath) during the special Fourth Meal. This action is reflective of the consciousness of the kabbalists, who were purposely using a highly potent sequence of words (*Shabbat Shalom*), which activates the Light of the Creator each time they are recited during the Sabbath. They chose to utter these words even though the Sabbath had already ended.

The kabbalists used this powerful expression to welcome the next Sabbath in at the precise moment the present Sabbath was ending. This was not about good manners. This was technology being utilized for the sole purpose of keeping those blackout curtains open, and to maintain a constant connection to the source' of all Divine Energy from one Sabbath to the next. Of course, the kabbalists knew that Friday evening and Saturday the Light was already theirs, courtesy of the spiritual laws of the cosmos. But they did everything in their power to keep that flame ablaze throughout the week.

And that's what makes a Kabbalist a Kabbalist.

I've seen my own father weep with sadness when Saturday evening arrived and the Sabbath ended. I remember specifically one time many years ago, when the Rav first explained to me why he was crying. I didn't understand it then. I had been looking forward to going to a movie as soon as possible that Saturday evening. I know now that the Rav wanted to share with me the extraordinary joy that fills one during this period.

I must admit I am still striving to become the spiritual beacon that my father has been for so many years. From an early age, I've known intellectually what the Sabbath offered me. During my youth, I enjoyed the Sabbath; there were many fulfilling and happy experiences. But looking back, I never felt the full impact of the energy that filled me to the point where my eyes welled with tears at its departure. I have prayed that one day, I, too, will share the full extent of my father's feelings. And I pray every day that the entire world will soon experience what the Rav experiences during this seventh day of the week, the day called the Sabbath.

I remember the Rav extending the Sabbath energy from Saturday night well past midnight, sometimes even until dawn of Sunday morning in order to keep the Sabbath glow alive. It wasn't just wishful thinking, or a refusal to say goodbye. According to the physics of the Sabbath, the Light remains until we, the participants, officially close it out anytime after sundown, using a few bits of kabbalistic technology. So the Rav would push the Sabbath late into Saturday evening by engaging in songs, dancing, prayer-connections, and some of the most amazing storytelling you ever heard. The Kabbalah Centre was a lot smaller in those days, and without a doubt, they were some of the happiest moments of my life.

I remember vividly the look on the faces of new friends of The Centre who had never observed a complete Sabbath before. For those who were new to such an experience, it could be quite overwhelming. By Saturday afternoon, the intensity of the experience challenged their basic comfort. The body would get restless. The ego got terribly uncomfortable. But I saw them fight through it. And by the time Saturday night arrived, when we were eating fresh hot pizzas, dancing, singing and telling stories to keep the Light of the Sabbath illuminated, these people were transformed, feeling higher than a kite deep inside. I was privileged to grow up in this kind of environment. It gratified me deeply to see my mother, Karen Berg, and the Rav give this opportunity to people from all over the world, people who never even knew something like the Sabbath existed.

Today, Kabbalah Centres around the world host many thousands of people for the Sabbath. And out of respect to the busy lives of our friends and congregants we adhere to a strict schedule. But in the days when The Centre was small, we would harness and extend the power of the Sabbath for well over thirty straight hours. I miss those days. But I am inspired by them to see the Light of the Sabbath stay ignited even longer— and finally to see it lit permanently, around the world, forever. This is what the age of the Messiah is about. It's non-stop pizza; it's dancing, singing, laughing, story telling and boundless bliss and joy beyond all imagining. It's joy without end.

Epilogue

THREE SECRET SHORTCUTS TO REDEMPTION

At the time of Creation, the Creator embedded in the code of the cosmos three secret short-cuts that could end the pain and suffering of the world *immediately*, by quickly restoring the energy and Light that illuminated during the time of Moses. The first short-cut has the power to create perfection without delay. It may sound simple—and it is—but once again it's not easy to achieve.

As we've learned throughout this book, each week over the last thirty-four centuries, humankind has had the opportunity to pour a little of the Light of Sinai back into the world on the Sabbath. The more people who participate in this day using the correct technology, the more quickly we will achieve the ultimate goal.

However, if humankind fails to achieve perfection by the seventh millennium, based on the Hebrew Calendar, the universe and cosmos will revert back into a state of paradise on its own. What does that mean? Where are we now, in terms of the time line?

In a nutshell, we are near the end of sixth millennium. In approximately, two hundred-plus years, we'll hit the seventh millennium and the world as we know it will no longer exist. It will transform into a highly-evolved civilization where *Love your Neighbor* will be the predominant consciousness permeating all of humanity.

However, the path to the seventh millennium becomes increasingly more painful and chaotic with each passing year. In other words, if we fail to achieve perfection through our own effort *before* the arrival of the seventh millennium, perfection will occur through considerable suffering. Why? In the absence of another stimulus, the torment we will experience will finally wake us up to the realization that self-interest and intolerance is an exercise in futility. In other words, we will learn the hard way.

If, however, we proactively achieve transformation before the arrival of the seventh millennium, we can lessen—even prevent—that pain and suffering, and attain the ultimate goal by way of mercy and kindness as opposed to harsh judgments. The longer it takes, the more painful the process. For this reason the Creator encrypted into the universe one particular shortcut that would allow *all* humankind to achieve perfection fast. Quickly. Instantly essentially, if just one congregation keeps two consecutive Sabbaths together in perfect unity and love, then the world will be redeemed. Chaos will come to an immediate end.

You might be wondering why two Sabbaths and not one. Essentially, you need the first Sabbath to transform yourself, to expose and root out all your negative traits so that the energy of the Sabbath can eradicate them. This will allow you to observe and connect on the second Sabbath with a perfect state of consciousness and in complete unity with everyone else. This means that you will have only love for your fellow participant during the Sabbath, and when everyone is filled with love for one another, they are totally unified.

These two Sabbaths are enough to redeem the entire world. That's the hidden secret and shortcut that's always available to us. It is so simple. So here—yet so far. Are we ready to ignite this power now? I know we are.

Which leads us to the second shortcut.

THE POWER OF THE ZOHAR

Kabbalists tell us that the Torah has both a body and a soul. The scroll is the body. So where is the soul? The great kabbalistic text called the *Zohar* is the soul of the Torah, containing the actual Light of immortality lost on Sinai. The Light that was infused inside the Tablets and inside the original Torah Scroll, is the exactly same Light that is released through the *Zohar*.

The original *Zohar* manuscripts, written by Rav Shimon Bar Yohai, were placed inside the original Ark approximately two thousand years ago by the kabbalists. These manuscripts were then discovered in the Middle Ages during the time of the Crusades when knights were excavating under the Temple in Jerusalem. The manuscripts were then taken to Spain, which was the main hub of kabbalistic study.

This is why the *Zohar* first appeared in Spain in the year 1290. The early kabbalists are clear on this matter. The appearance of the *Zohar* in the world is equivalent to the appearance of immortality on Mount Sinai. Both embody the full revelation of the Light. And the more people who access and utilize the *Zohar*, the faster we replenish the power and energy that we lost on Mount Sinai.

Incorporating the *Zohar* into one's life is, unquestionably, the most powerful way to activate the power of the Sabbath. Even more amazingly, it gives us the ability to access the power of the Sabbath during the rest of the week!

How is that possible?

The Torah is governed by the laws of physical reality. Physical reality is governed by the laws of time. Thus the Torah's Sabbath Energy only becomes activated on Saturday, a specific time frame and window in which we can capture this Divine Force. However, the *Zohar* is above time and space. The *Zohar*, being the soul of the Torah, is not governed by the physical laws.

In other words, the body is under the constraints of time. The soul is not. Ergo, the Torah is under the constraints of time and the *Zohar* is not. For this reason, we can access the *Zohar*'s power seven days a week. When we combine *both* the Torah and the *Zohar* in our lives, we literally tap into the energy of immortality and transformation at the highest, most extreme levels imaginable.

The Power of the Righteous Sage

The third shortcut is to get as many people as possible, throughout the world, to make some sort of kabbalistic connection to the Sabbath each week from wherever they are.

Many centuries ago, when travel was limited to walking, or hitching up your horse, people would travel for weeks and even months just to spend one Sabbath with a genuine kabbalist. People would travel hundreds and thousands of miles to attend one Sabbath in the Ukrainian village of Meziboz, to be with the great Kabbalist Rav Israel ben Eliezer (Baal Shem Tov).

Why? When a congregation of people gather to connect to the Sabbath, everyone, regardless of his or her personal situation, ascends as high as the most righteous and purest person among them. Therefore, spending a Sabbath with a great kabbalist insured that the participants reached the highest levels of the spiritual world through the merit of the righteous sage.

The Kabbalah Centres around the world are still connected to, and guided by the original founders, Rav Yehuda Ashlag and Rav Brandwein. Though not present with us on a physical level, their connection to The Centre, and their leadership is that much stronger for they are closer to true reality, the realm of pure consciousness. Every teacher in The Centre is connected to these great souls and for that reason, Sabbath at a Kabbalah Centre anywhere in the world, no matter how large or small the facility, elevates us to the highest possible level.

The most profound impact upon the Sabbath at The Kabbalah Centre is the consciousness of the Rav and my mother, Karen, who took the unprecedented step of opening up the doors of Kabbalah and The Centre to anyone, regardless of their faith, race, background or past history. The consciousness of true unconditional love, zero judgment, combined with a fervent desire to truly empower the world with the Light of the *Zohar* through the power of the Sabbath permeates every Centre around the world.

The Universal Sabbath

As noted earlier, Muslims observe the Sabbath on Friday. Christians observe the Sabbath on Sunday. And the Israelites connect on Saturday. According to Kabbalah, all three Sabbaths help us transform the world and bring us a step closer to the ultimate Redemption and perfection of the world. This is a perfect manifestation of the Three Column System.

However, unbeknownst to most people throughout history, the energy and Light that is revealed on Saturday is not exclusive to the Israelites. It belongs to everyone. Therefore it has the power to enrich, enhance, and magnify *exponentially* the Sabbath energy of Friday and Sunday, as well. That's right. Using the tools of Kabbalah, a Muslim and a Christian can observe their respective Sabbath but they can also make a connection on Saturday to tap into the Light and Energy that radiates from the 99 Percent Reality.

The whole idea behind this universal component of the Saturday Sabbath connection is to bring together all of humankind to achieve that ultimate threshold and critical mass of humanity necessary to tip the scales from darkness to Light, from imperfection to perfection. Make no mistake. This is a race against time. The sooner we unleash the full power of the Sabbath and the *Zohar*, the sooner we achieve the perfection that will make every individual human being on Earth happy beyond all calculation.

For thirty-four centuries the ideas presented in this book were kept secret, and therefore, unknown to humankind. For that reason, the race never really got started but the clock still kept on ticking. This is the underlying reason behind all those centuries of suffering, persecution and war.

But now, with the publication of this book, with its secrets and tools, we can make a dash for the finish line and transform our world peacefully, gracefully, and mercifully.

MORE BOOKS THAT CAN HELP YOU BRING THE WISDOM OF KABBALAH INTO YOUR LIFE

The Way of the Kabbalist: A User's Guide to Technology for the Soul
By Yehuda Berg

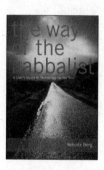

What is Kabbalah? This complete reference for anyone interested in the practices of The Kabbalah Centre defines and explains the meaning behind what might seem like mysterious rituals to the uninformed, but are actually tools anyone can use to achieve positive goals and transformation. By the author of *The Power of Kabbalah*.

Genesis: The Kabbalistic Bible, Volume 1
Edited by Yehuda Berg

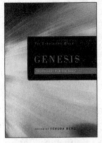

The first in a projected five-volume series presents Kabbalah's interpretation of the First Book of Moses, in a user-friendly format, with Hebrew and English printed on facing pages, and running from front to back. Edited and with contemporary insights by Yehuda Berg, who was recently named one of America's Top Rabbis in Newsweek Magazine, the text is complemented by excerpts from the *Zohar* and from the writings of history's greatest kabbalists.

The Wisdom of Truth: 12 Essays by the Holy Kabbalist Rav Yehuda Ashlag
Edited by Michael Berg

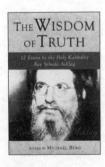

All of the essential truths of Kabbalah are encapsulated in these thought-provoking essays by arguably the most profound mystic of the 20th century. Originally published in 1984 as *Kabbalah: A Gift of the Bible*, and long out of print, this is a new translation from the Hebrew, edited and with an introduction by noted Kabbalah scholar Michael Berg.

The Secret History of the Zohar
By Michael Berg

This concise overview of Kabbalah's influence on great figures in the arts and sciences throughout the ages, including Plato, the Knights Templar, Christopher Columbus, Sir Isaac Newton, and Carl Jung, demonstrates that the *Zohar* has never been simply for scholars of Judaism. By the author of the bestseller (WSJ), *The Way*.

The Prayer of the Kabbalist: The 42 - Letter Name of God
By Yehuda Berg

According to the ancient wisdom of Kabbalah, the powerful prayer known as *Ana Bekho'ah* invokes The 42-Letter Name of God, which connects to no less than the undiluted force of creation. By tapping into this connection through the Prayer, you can leave the past behind and make a fresh start. If you recite the Prayer on a regular basis, you are able to use the force of Creation to create miracles, both in your everyday life and in the world at large. This book explains the meaning behind the 42 letters and gives you practical steps for how best to connect to their power.

Secrets of the Zohar: Stories and Meditations to Awaken the Heart
By Michael Berg

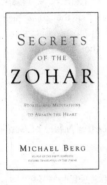

The *Zohar*'s secrets are the secrets of the Bible, passed on as oral tradition and then recorded as a sacred text that remained hidden for thousands of years. They have never been revealed quite as they are here in these pages, which decipher the codes behind the best stories of the ancient sages and offer a special meditation for each one. Entire portions of the *Zohar* are presented, with the Aramaic and its English translation in side-by-side columns. This allows you to scan and to read aloud so that you can draw on the *Zohar*'s full energy and achieve spiritual transformation. Open this book and open your heart to the Light of the *Zohar*!

Days of Connection: A Guide to Kabbalah's Holidays and New Moons
By Michael Berg

The ancient wisdom of Kabbalah teaches that each month of the lunar year holds different opportunities for us to grow and change and, conversely, holds unique pitfalls for getting stalled on our journey toward spiritual transformation. The special power of each month is strongest at its beginning, the time of the new moon, known as Rosh Chodesh. And holidays are unmatched as windows in time that make specific kinds of spiritual energy available to us. In *Days of Connection*, Michael Berg guides us through the kabbalistic calendar and explains the meaning and power behind all of these special days.

The 72 Names of God: Technology for the Soul™
By Yehuda Berg

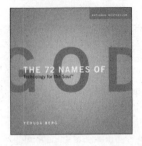

The 72 Names of God are not "names" in any ordinary sense, but a state-of-the-art technology that deeply touches the human soul and is the key to ridding yourself of depression, stress, stagnation, anger, and many other emotional and physical problems. The Names represent a connection to the infinite spiritual current that flows through the universe. When you correctly bring these power sources together, you are able to gain control over your life and transform it for the better.

The Power of Kabbalah
By Yehuda Berg

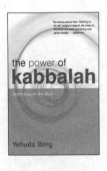

Imagine your life filled with unending joy, purpose, and contentment. Imagine your days infused with pure insight and energy. This is *The Power of Kabbalah*. It is the path from the momentary pleasure that most of us settle for, to the lasting fulfillment that is yours to claim. Your deepest desires are waiting to be realized. Find out how, in this basic introduction to the ancient wisdom of Kabbalah.

THE ZOHAR

Composed more than 2,000 years ago, the *Zohar* is a set of 23 books, a commentary on biblical and spiritual matters in the form of conversations among spiritual masters. But to describe the *Zohar* only in physical terms is greatly misleading. In truth, the *Zohar* is nothing less than a powerful tool for achieving the most important purposes of our lives. It was given to all humankind by the Creator to bring us protection, to connect us with the Creator's Light, and ultimately to fulfill our birthright of true spiritual transformation.

More than eighty years ago, when The Kabbalah Centre was founded, the *Zohar* had virtually disappeared from the world. Few people in the general population had ever heard of it. Whoever sought to read it—in any country, in any language, at any price—faced a long and futile search.

Today all this has changed. Through the work of The Kabbalah Centre and the editorial efforts of Michael Berg, the *Zohar* is now being brought to the world, not only in the original Aramaic language but also in English. The new English *Zohar* provides everything for connecting to this sacred text on all levels: the original Aramaic text for scanning; an English translation; and clear, concise commentary for study and learning.

THE KABBALAH CENTRE®

The Kabbalah Centre® is a spiritual organization dedicated to bringing the wisdom of Kabbalah to the world. The Kabbalah Centre® itself has existed for more than 80 years, but its spiritual lineage extends back to Rav Isaac Luria in the 16th century and even further back to Rav Shimon bar Yochai, who revealed the principal text of Kabbalah, the Zohar, more than 2,000 years ago.

The Kabbalah Centre® was founded in 1922 by Rav Yehuda Ashlag, one of the greatest kabbalists of the 20th Century. When Rav Ashlag left this world, leadership of The Kabbalah Centre® was taken on by Rav Yehuda Brandwein. Before his passing, Rav Brandwein designated Rav Berg as director of The Kabbalah Centre®. Now, for more than 30 years, The Kabbalah Centre® has been under the direction of Rav Berg, his wife Karen Berg, and their sons, Yehuda Berg and Michael Berg.

Although there are many scholarly studies of Kabbalah, The Kabbalah Centre® does not teach Kabbalah as an academic discipline but as a way of creating a better life. The mission of The Kabbalah Centre® is to make the practical tools and spiritual teachings of Kabbalah available and accessible to everyone regardless of religion, ethnicity, gender or age.

The Kabbalah Centre® makes no promises. But if people are willing to work hard to grow and become actively sharing, caring and tolerant human beings, Kabbalah teaches that they will then experience fulfillment and joy in a way previously unknown to them. This sense of fulfillment, however, comes gradually and is always the result of the student's spiritual work.

Our ultimate goal is for all humanity to gain the happiness and fulfillment that is our true destiny.

Kabbalah teaches its students to question and test everything they learn. One of the most important teachings of Kabbalah is that there is no coercion in spirituality.

What Does The Kabbalah Centre® Offer?

Local Kabbalah Centres around the world offer onsite lectures, classes, study groups, holiday celebrations and services, and a community of teachers and fellow students. To find a Centre near you, go to www.kabbalah.com.

For those of you unable to access a physical Kabbalah Centre due to the constraints of location or time, we have other ways to participate in The Kabbalah Centre® community.

At www.kabbalah.com, we feature online blogs, newsletters, weekly wisdom, a store, and much more.

It's a wonderful way to stay tuned in and in touch, and it gives you access to programs that will expand your mind and challenge you to continue your spiritual work.

Student Support

The Kabbalah Centre® empowers people to take responsibility for their own lives. It's about the teachings, not the teachers. But on your journey to personal growth, things can be unclear and sometimes rocky, so it is helpful to have a coach or teacher. Simply call 1 800 KABBALAH toll free.

All Student Support instructors have studied Kabbalah under the direct supervision of Kabbalist Rav Berg, widely recognized as the preeminent kabbalist of our time.

We have also created opportunities for you to interact with other Student Support students through study groups, monthly connections, holiday retreats, and other events held around the country.

Wishing my family and friends the merit to learn
Kabbalah and to believe in immortality.

Immortality is the true key to revealing Mashiach.

I also want to express gratitude to The Rav,
Karen and family.